PROPHET AT THE GATE

PROPHET AT THE GATE

Norman Murray Bell
and the Quest for Peace

Wayne Facer

Blackstone Editions

Blackstone Editions
Toronto, Ontario, Canada
www.BlackstoneEditions.com

© 2021 by Wayne Facer
All rights reserved

978-1-7753556-5-6

Library and Archives Canada Cataloguing in Publication

Title: Prophet at the gate : Norman Murray Bell and the quest for peace / Wayne Facer.
Names: Facer, W. A. P., author.
Description: Includes bibliographical references and index.
Identifiers: Canadiana (print) 20210172878 | Canadiana (ebook) 20210172916 | ISBN 9781775355656 (softcover) | ISBN 9781775355663 (EPUB)
Subjects: LCSH: Bell, N. M. (Norman Murray), 1887-1962. | LCSH: Pacifists—New Zealand—Biography. | LCSH: Peace movements—New Zealand—History—20th century. | LCGFT: Biographies.
Classification: LCC JZ5540.2.B45 F33 2021 | DDC 327.1/72092—dc23

Front cover image: Caspar David Friedrich, *Monastery Graveyard in the Snow*. The painting was destroyed by air raids during World War II and only a black and white photograph survives. Source: Wikiart Visual Art Encyclopaedia.

For Gareth and Aena

Let the Māori karakia (prayer)
speak to the human family

Let peace reign   Kia tau te rangimārie
on all the people of the world Ki runga i ngā iwi o te ao

Contents

Illustrations	ix
Foreword *by Peter Lineham*	xiv
Timeline	xvi
Introduction	1
1. A Dissenting Heritage and the Challenge of Orthodoxy Albertland, Auckland and Christchurch, 1862-1909	15

2. Intellectual Development
  University Life and Religious Study
  in Britain and the Continent, 1909-1916
	33

3. War and Resistance
  Theology, Conscientious Objection,
  Imprisonment and Return to Society, 1916-1919
	53

4. Working for Peace Movements Against War and Fascism, 1921-1939	70
5. The Second World War and Its Aftermath, 1940-1962	100
Afterword: Larry Ross and Nuclear-Free New Zealand	127
Acknowledgements	143

Appendixes
  1. Voyages of the Albertland Ships
  2. Map of the Albertland Settlement
	
	148
	150

Contents

3. Descendants of James and Henrietta Bell	152
4. Free Religious Movement Lectures, 1934-1944	154
Notes	166
Bibliography	184
Index	198

Illustrations

George Clarendon Beale, Untitled (Parihaka and Mount Taranaki), 1881	3
Collection of Puke Ariki, New Plymouth. TM2000.245	
First Albertlanders leave for New Zealand	14
Albertland Museum and Heritage Centre	
Farewell to *Matilda Wattenbach*	14
Albertland Museum and Heritage Centre	
Rev. William Rawson Brame	16
Albertland Museum and Heritage Centre	
Rev. Samuel Edger	16
Albertland Museum and Heritage Centre	
Vessels loading timber at Port Albert	18
Albertland Museum and Heritage Centre	
Dr James Bell and Mrs Henrietta Bell	20
Albertland Museum and Heritage Centre	
Sarah Jerome Becroft	21
Albertland Museum and Heritage Centre	
Annie Bell with her three sons wearing Bell clan kilts, c.1902	24
Norman Murray Bell Papers, Christchurch City Libraries, ANZC Archives, Archive 280	

Illustrations

Christ's College, Christchurch — 26
Obtained from the collection, and used with permission of, Christchurch City Libraries, File Reference CCL PhotoCD17, ING 0018

River Avon, Christchurch — 28

Norman Murray Bell and friend, London, 1910 — 34
Norman Murray Bell Papers, Christchurch City Libraries, ANZC Archives, Archive 280

Professor Francis Haslam — 35
A History of the University of Canterbury (Christchurch: University of Canterbury, 1973)

William Whetham — 35
Trinity College Chapel, Cambridge

Ernest Rutherford — 36
The Cavendish Laboratory, University of Cambridge

Charles Chilton — 36
Creative Commons 4.0 International License. Transactions and Proceedings of the Royal Society of New Zealand, vol. 60 (1930)

John Maynard Keynes — 37

Bertrand Russell — 37

Charles Voysey — 42

Walter Walsh — 42
Unknown photographer, Walter Walsh by Lafayette © National Portrait Gallery, London. 24 July 1928. With permission

Alfred Holt — 44
Courtesy of Liverpool City Council Libraries & Archives

Muspratt Laboratory, Liverpool University — 45

United College courtyard, St Andrews University — 47
Creative Commons 2.0 Jared & Corin

Andrew Carnegie — 48

Illustrations

Professor James Irvine   49
    Norman Murray Bell Papers, Christchurch City Libraries,
    ANZC Archives, Archive 280

War Workers, Chemical Laboratory,   50
St Andrews University, summer 1915
    Norman Murray Bell Papers, Christchurch City Libraries,
    ANZC Archives, Archive 280

University of Bern, Main Building   51
    Creative Commons 3.0 Bobo 11

Norman Murray Bell and his brother Harold   54
    Norman Murray Bell Papers, Christchurch City Libraries,
    ANZC Archives, Archive 280

Albert Schweitzer   57
    Wikimedia Commons, Creative Commons 3.0 license

Rotoaira Prison Camp   65
    Acting Jailer Roto Aira forwarding photos of Whaka-
    Papanui bridge [ACGS 1665 202/1918/8/6] Archives
    New Zealand The Department of Internal Affairs Te Tari
    Taiwhenua.

John A. Lee   66

The No More War Committee, c. 1930   71
    Courtesy Efford family & Voices Against War website
    identifier VAW 083

Third New Zealand Esperanto Congress, Christchurch, 1931   72
    Photo provided by Brent Efford

Chancery Lane, Christchurch, 1932   73
    James Fitzgerald, Chancery Lane, Christchurch, New
    Zealand. Collection of Christchurch Art Gallery Te Puna o
    Waiwhetū; 2011, reproduced with permission.

West Christchurch District High School   75
Ensom Essay competition winners
    The Press, 6 October 1931, p. 11. NLNZ, https://paperspast.
    natlib.govt.nz/newspapers/CHP19311006.2.83.3

Frank B. Kellogg and Aristide Briand   76

Illustrations

Frederick and Esther Sinclaire — 77

Peace march, c.1937 — 81
   Norman Murray Bell Papers, Christchurch City Libraries, ANZC Archives, Archive 280

Ursula Bethell — 82
   Ursula Bethell Papers (MB558, Ref 16144) Macmillan Brown Library, Christchurch, New Zealand

Rita Angus painting self portrait, 1936-1937, by Jean Bertram. — 83
   Te Papa Tongarewa Museum of New Zealand (CA000242/001/0001)

Cambridge Terrace apartments — 84
   With permission of Canterbury Museum, 1984.272.2

Ian Milner, Denis Glover and Robert Lowry — 85
   Courtesy Alexander Turnbull Library. Reference Number: 1/2-075453-F

Rev. James Chapple — 87
   Auckland War Memorial Museum Library, Auckland Unitarian Church collection

Socialist Sunday School wagon trip, Auckland, 1920s — 89
   Ref: 1/2-002175-F. Alexander Turnbull Library, Wellington, New Zealand. /records/23125109. Reproduced with permission

Douglas Lilburn conducting the National Symphony Orchestra, 1948 — 101
   Archives New Zealand, Creative Commons 2.0

Lincoln Efford — 105
   Photo provided by Brent Efford

Portrait of Blanche Edith Baughan by Clifford — 115
   Photo provided by the National Library of Australia
   https://nla.gov.au/nla.obj-136622944

Norman Murray Bell outside his house, c.1950 — 116
   Norman Murray Bell Papers, Christchurch City Libraries, ANZC Archives, Archive 280

Norman Murray Bell and a friend on a cycling trip, 1950s   117
    Norman Murray Bell Papers, Christchurch City Libraries,
    ANZC Archives, Archive 280

Hiroshima Day march, August 6, 1961   119
    Photo provided by Brent Efford

Rev. Professor Sir Lloyd Geering becoming a Member   122
of the Order of New Zealand, 2007
    With permission of Stuff/Dominion Post

Young Larry Ross   129
    Courtesy of Laurie Ross and the New Zealand Nuclear Free
    Zone Peacemaking Association

Bertrand Russell   132
    Courtesy of Laurie Ross, Nuclear Free Peacemakers .org.nz

Larry Ross with the logo he designed for Nuclear Free   137
New Zealand, 1992
    Courtesy of Laurie Ross and the New Zealand Nuclear Free
    Zone Peacemaking Association

Stuart Macaskill   138
    Courtesy of Patricia Macaskill

Elspeth Vallance   140

Derek McCullough   141

Mayor of Christchurch awarding Larry Ross   142
the Christchurch Peace City award, 2002

The *Matilda Wattenbach* leaving England, 1862   149
    Albertland Museum and Heritage Centre

Foreword

The life of Norman Murray Bell is surely one of the most moving stories in modern New Zealand history. This biography is so moving and compelling that readers will wonder why this name is not as familiar as those of Archibald Baxter, or Ormond Burton, or even Te Whiti O Rongomai. Norman Bell's courage, foresight and depth of experience are profound, yet he has been largely forgotten. So we are deeply in the debt of Wayne Facer for making this story more accessible and revealing its richness.

Norman Murray Bell won high respect at first because of his academic brilliance. From his very ordinary background, he gained scholarships to Christ's College and Canterbury University College and then gained a scholarship to Cambridge. Wayne Facer has been able to fill in many of the gaps in the story of the next few years, tracing his links with sundry Chemistry laboratories, and the recognition he received also in the Arts and Theology. He was truly a polymath.

After he returned to New Zealand his deep principles led him to refuse to take the easy way out of war service. He paid a high price, indeed a higher price than most, because he was an intellectual and the opportunities for employment were therefore limited. He was thereafter evidently dismissed by many as an eccentric. That must have been acutely painful to a man who had pondered issues so deeply.

Wayne has traced with superb care the very different world that Bell subsequently contributed to. He was active in socialist, radical religious and reformist circles, mingling with a brilliant circle of artists, writers and musicians. People like Lincoln Efford, Frederick Sinclaire, Archibald Barrington, Douglas Lilburn and Rita Angus were a significant circle of people who contributed very profoundly to New Zealand culture.

I can hardly appreciate the pain for Bell that he was not able to make a contribution for which he was so equipped. Yet I am impressed at the new opportunities he found to contribute to New Zealand, in fighting for the rights of the Māori and Samoan peoples, in arguing for a richer concept of pacifism and in advocating vegetarianism.

So this is an important biography, which needs to find its way onto the shelves of every school and public library. The author is tentative about calling Norman Murray Bell a prophet, but in my view, he exactly reflects the burden of the prophetic tradition. For fundamentally those prophets courageously exposed sin and hypocrisy and exposed the behaviour of their people in the light of a plumbline of right values. Bell played such a role among the New Zealanders of his day, and the way he was treated exposes their deficiencies. I hope very much that this biography may restore Bell's reputation as a great New Zealander, and congratulate the author for his invaluable work.

Peter Lineham, PhD MNZM
Professor Emeritus of History
Massey University

Timeline

1862	September 8: Dr James and Henrietta Bell, Norman Murray Bell's grandparents, arrive in Auckland on the *Matilda Wattenbach* as part of the nonconformist Albertland settlers.
1863	Horace Roland Bell is born in Port Albert, father Dr James Bell and mother Henrietta Mary Bell.
1870	August 9: James Bell dies at Port Albert aged 34 years.
1883	Horace Roland Bell begins work at the Railways Department in Auckland.
1886	March 11: Horace Roland Bell, eldest son of the late Dr James and Henrietta Bell, is married to Annie Coffey, second daughter of the late Samuel Coffey of Glasgow. Rev. W. Gittos performed the ceremony in the Lincoln Street, Ponsonby, home of the groom's uncle, Harold James Bell.
1887	January 28: Norman Murray Bell is born in Avondale; his father Horace is a Railway Stationmaster.
1891	January 8: Horace Roland Bell is presented with a "handsome testimonial" by the residents of Huntly, where he has been stationmaster, as he leaves to take charge of the Te Aroha Railway Station.
1896	May 11: Horace Bell, stationmaster at Paeroa, is appointed clerk in the District Traffic Manager's office in Auckland. Norman Murray Bell attends Parnell District School.

Timeline

1898	A Parliamentary committee is set up to improve connections between trains and ships, particularly on the Wellington to Lyttelton steamer service. Improved connections with other provinces are considered and the Minister of Railways joins the committee.
1899	Horace Bell is promoted to the Lyttelton Station at the Port; serves there for nineteen years. The family moves from Auckland. Norman Bell attends West Lyttelton School, Standard VI, is Dux boy and gains a scholarship to Christ's College, initially for two years.
1900-1904	Norman Murray Bell attends Christ's College, becoming Head of School (equal to Dux, a term not used at Christ's College), winning many form prizes, the Tancred prizes for Literature and History, and the Balfour prize for Divinity.
1905	Norman Murray Bell secures a Junior University Scholarship, placing third in the country. A half day holiday is held at Christ's College in honour of his success.
1905-1909	Norman Murray Bell attends Canterbury University College, graduates BA in 1908, Senior Scholar in Greek and qualifies for a Scholarship in Chemistry from the University of New Zealand. Graduates in 1909 from the University of New Zealand MA with First Class Honours in Classics and Second Class Honours in Chemistry.
1909	Defence Act introduces compulsory military training for young men and schoolboys. The Act allows exemption from training on religious grounds, but not conscientious objection, subject to the approval of the Military authorities. Training is required for Junior Cadets aged 12-14, Cadets aged 14-18 and young men aged 18 to 21 (later extended to 25) in the Territorial Reserve until 30 years.

Norman Murray Bell leaves on a National Research Scholarship for Trinity College, University of Cambridge in the UK. |
| **1910** | Norman Murray Bell's paper "On the Velocity of Evolution of Oxygen from Bleaching Powder Solutions in the Presence of Cobalt-Nitrate and the Modifications produced by the Additions of Various Compounds", first presented to the |

Timeline

1910
(continued) Philosophical Institute of Canterbury, is published in *Transactions and Proceedings of the Royal Society of New Zealand* 43 (1910), pp. 26-28.

1909-1912 Norman Murray Bell completes his BA in classics at Trinity College, Cambridge, and wins the College Classics prize.

1912 The Defence Act removes the compulsory training of Junior Cadets aged 12-14 years.

1913 April 15: Henrietta Mary Bell, grandmother of Norman Bell, dies.

1913-1914 Norman Murray Bell is a Chemistry Research Student in residence at the University of Liverpool.

1914-1915 Norman Murray Bell is Research Student in Chemistry and Education at St Andrews University, and is awarded the Education Medal. With Alfred Holt he has a paper published in the *Journal of the Chemical Society Transactions* in 1914; and a paper published in the *Transactions of the Faraday Society* in 1915.

1915 Norman Murray Bell graduates Bachelor of Divinity (with credit towards one paper at honours level) in Theology from the University of London.

In October the New Zealand National Registration Act is passed, requiring eligible men to state whether they would volunteer for overseas service, undertake civil service in New Zealand, or do neither.

1915-1916 Norman Murray Bell is enrolled as a candidate in philosophy at the University of Bern.

1916 August 1: Military Service Act introduced in New Zealand. The volunteer system remained with conscription to be used in areas where the quota of recruits was insufficient.

The New Zealand Labour Party is formed in July. The New Zealand Section of the Women's International League for Peace and Freedom is formed in Auckland.

1917 March 1: Norman Murray Bell returns to New Zealand and is appointed assistant master and demonstrator in physics at Christchurch Boys High School.

Timeline

1917 (continued)	August 28: Norman Murray Bell is arrested for breaching the Military Service Act, and sentenced to 28 days detention. October 13: Norman Murray Bell is sentenced to two years in prison with hard labour for disobeying a lawful command.
1919	Released from prison in April, Norman Murray Bell resumes educational coaching. He is an advocate for the Conscientious Objectors' Fellowship, lobbying to free those conscientious objectors still in prison after the end of the war. He accepts an invitation to join the National Peace Council. He is appointed tutor in sociology for the Canterbury Workers' Educational Association.
1922	Horace Roland Bell retires on superannuation after 39 years as a Railways Department servant, working in both the shipping and railways side at Lyttelton. He is presented with a silver cake dish and a gavel.
1923	Norman Murray Bell unsuccessfully nominated as a national vice president of the New Zealand Labour Party, at the Dominion Conference held in April in Christchurch.
1925	Norman Murray Bell and Rev. Clyde Carr take charge of the Unitarian Progressive Society (Christchurch Unitarian church) following the retirement of Rev. James Chapple. When Carr goes into politics in 1927 Bell has sole charge and changes the society into the Free Religious Movement.
1928	February 19: Lincoln Efford helps Fred Page form the No More War Movement, which declares "war is a crime against humanity". Norman Murray Bell completes *Maori myths and rites in the light of human ontogeny: a physiologico-psychical contribution to the study of religious origins*. It is recorded in the Canterbury University College catalogue as a D. Litt. Thesis.
1930	Following Fred Page's death, Norman Murray Bell and Baptist minister Charles Cole assume leadership of the No More War Movement. December 5: Norman Murray Bell experiences a profound psychological event, after which he understands the web of life that unites all living things and from then on is a devoted vegetarian.

Timeline

1931	January 12: Norman Murray Bell gives a radio talk on station 3YA on "Esperanto".
	Norman Murray Bell is elected Chairman of the No More War Movement.
	October: Norman Murray Bell gives a talk to the Practical Psychology Club entitled "Hallucination or Illumination: Psychology of Ecstatic Vision", based on the event of 5 December 1930.
1932	December 27: Norman Murray Bell is elected vice-president of the New Zealand Esperanto Society at its fourth Congress held at Masterton.
1933	Branches of the Movement Against War and Fascism have been formed in Auckland, Wellington, Christchurch and Dunedin.
	Norman Murray Bell is appointed Esperanto tutor for the Canterbury Workers' Educational Association and Professor Frederick Sinclaire tutor in Literature.
1934	A national congress of the Movement Against War is held in Wellington.
1935	August 29: Annie McQuirk Bell, mother of Norman Murray Bell, dies in Christchurch and is buried in the Bromley cemetery.
	October 4: Norman Murray Bell, in his role as president of the Humanitarian and Anti-Vivisection Society, gives a radio talk on station 3YA "The Cause of the Animals".
1936	Norman Murray Bell is appointed to temporary academic position in the Department of Classics at Canterbury University College, doing relieving work for the second and third terms.
	The Humanitarian and Anti-Vivisection Society moves into the rooms of the No More War Movement in Chancery Lane; volunteers staff the office all week.
1936-1940	Norman Murray Bell returns to Canterbury University College as a student studying Psychology, Māori and Hebrew.

Timeline

1939-1940 October 1939: As war breaks out, a Combined Pacifist Committee, led by Norman Murray Bell, Charles Mackie, the Anglican couple Kathleen and Thurlow Thompson, Lincoln Efford and the Quaker John Johnson, keep public meetings going till January 1940. Efford runs the Co-operative Pacifist Press until the press is confiscated in June 1940.

1940 National Service Emergency Regulations passed to introduce national military conscription for all males between 18 and 46, although no soldier under 21 could serve overseas. Subject to military requirements, manpower control to direct labour into essential industries introduced.

1941 Teachers (Conscientious and Defaulters) Emergency Regulations, remain in force until 1948. A teacher who appeals on conscientious grounds against conscription or is convicted of being a defaulter is automatically placed on unpaid leave of absence.

1943 Government Service (Defaulters) Emergency Regulations introduced, which dismisses a military service defaulter from any Government employment. The Electoral Emergency Regulations of 1943 removes anyone convicted of being a military service defaulter from the electoral roll. This remains in force until the passing of the Emergency Regulations Amendment Act of 1950.

1945 September 14: Horace Roland Bell, father of Norman Murray Bell, dies at Christchurch and is buried at Bromley cemetery.

1946 Women's International League for Peace and Freedom stops functioning in New Zealand.

Norman Murray Bell refuses to allow the much depleted No More War Movement to amalgamate with the Peace Council, arguing that a number of separate organisations could achieve more than one umbrella organisation.

1949 Norman Murray Bell is conferred with his MA degree by the University of Cambridge.

1962 August 5: Norman Murray Bell dies at Princess Margaret Hospital, Christchurch and is cremated at Bromley cemetery.

Introduction

The subject of this study is Norman Murray Bell (1887-1962), an outstanding New Zealander who has all but disappeared from the national consciousness. In his time he was the head student at the country's oldest and most prestigious Church of England school, Christ's College in Christchurch. From there he went to Canterbury University College, then part of the University of New Zealand, where he completed a double major in Classics and Chemistry for his BA and then undertook an MA degree with first-class honours. His classics professor arranged an inaugural scholarship for a New Zealand student to study at Trinity College, Cambridge University, which Bell received in 1909. This scholarship also had the financial support of the New Zealand government.

By all accounts, Bell developed into a polymath, perhaps New Zealand's first from the colonial academic world, excelling in science and arts as well as theology, conducting research into education and chemistry and also studying philosophy of science. He was fluent in several languages, including German, French, Hebrew, Greek, Latin and Māori. The term polymath is associated with the ideal of Renaissance Humanism, which aspired to the acquisition of almost all the available important knowledge in the areas of science, the arts, and social and artistic development. A similar term derived from Renaissance Humanism is *Homo Universalis* or *Uomo Universale*, which means the universal person or man. Today the term polymath refers to profoundly based knowledge with a high proficiency or accomplishment over different subjects. It is important to distinguish this from genius: Albert Einstein and Marie Curie are widely regarded as geniuses, but they were not polymaths. Bell, as his story unfolds, clearly comes within this ambit. His breadth of knowledge in the fields of science, education, philosophy, theology and languages reflects the ideal of the Renaissance man.

But what of the claim that he should be regarded as a prophet? There is the traditional Biblical use of the term to mean a person inspired to proclaim the will of God, but this is not the light in which Norman Murray Bell was seen by his contemporaries, nor was this how he saw himself. For him prophecy was speaking truth in the face of power; he stood in his community fighting for good against evil, justice against injustice. He can be regarded as a prophet in the modern sense of the term: as a person who speaks in a visionary way about a cause. His cause was peace. His life provides a window into the peace movement in New Zealand, particularly during the period between the two world wars. As will be seen, he was a prophet without honour in his own country.[1]

Parihaka and the Origins of the Modern Peace Movement

The appreciation of pacifism and the peace movement within New Zealand's religious, social, and military historiography is growing and developing in significance each year. New Zealand had its own momentous event in the late nineteenth century that was largely overlooked until about fifty years ago: the establishment of a Māori community based upon principles of pacifism and civil disobedience.

In 1866, two Māori prophets, Te Whiti-o-Rongomai (c.1832-1907) and Tohu Kākahi (1828-1907) established the Māori community of Parihaka in the shadow of Mount Taranaki. They preached and practised non-violent resistance in response to the confiscation of their lands and associated legal and political oppression. Theirs was a unique Christian worldview, a blend of the Old Testament prophets with a pacifist component based on the principles of the Sermon on the Mount. Parihaka became the largest Māori settlement in the country. The villagers ploughed lands and removed survey pegs in symbolic repossession of their land.

Introduction

George Clarendon Beale, Untitled (Parihaka and Mount Taranaki), 1881

In 1881, the peaceful village of Parihaka was invaded by 1,600 militia and armed constabulary ordered in by the government while the Governor was out of the country. The villagers offered no resistance to the invaders. Many villagers were sent back to their home areas. The leaders were imprisoned, houses and crops were destroyed, women were raped, and the government suspended the legal rights of prisoners. With rare exceptions, there was little condemnation of this outrage from the churches and civil society. Reports of the attack were published in newspapers in Australia, the United States of America and Great Britain. While none were condemnatory of the violence inflicted on the Māori pacifists, a report in the American press contained an amazing admission:

> What tried the resources of the Government most was the refusal of Te Whiti to resort to violence. Life and property, except the property represented in the new roads, he uniformly respected, and cared only to plow up the turnpikes and build his fences across them. Now it appears that the Government has caused Te Whiti himself to be arrested, and, in accordance with his policy of peaceful measures and his belief that his mission is divine, he has offered no resistance.[2]

Introduction

However, the events of 1881 did not end Parihaka as a village. It continued as a centre of non-violent resistance to settler laws until the deaths of both Te Whiti and Tohu in 1907. While their dream of peace and harmony was not achieved, they avoided full-scale war at a time when such an outbreak seemed likely, a remarkable achievement. The spirit of the prophets of Parihaka lived on: an Irish delegation visiting New Zealand went to Parihaka and later had a meeting with Mahatma Gandhi (1869-1948). Gandhi's grandson, Dr Arun Gandhi, confirmed that what Gandhi learnt about Parihaka at this meeting helped him develop his own non-violent resistance plans.[3] Following from the success of Gandhi's campaign for Indian independence in 1947 was the effect it had on Martin Luther King Jr (1929-1968). In 1959 King visited India to learn about Gandhi's ideals and strategies. He met many members of Gandhi's family and stated that Gandhi was his "guiding light." Thus the Parihaka story spread to the other side of the world, where it influenced great changes in India, South Africa and the United States of America and continues to this day to be a beacon for peace. In 2000, the United Nations' International Year for a Culture of Peace, two Parihaka kuia (elderly women), Parekaitu Tito and Sadie Rukuwai, were each presented with a UNESCO Peace-builder Award. In 2003 Parihaka was visited by an international delegation of representatives of Martin Luther King Jr, Mahatma Gandhi and Daisaku Ikeda, a Japanese Buddhist peace campaigner. It continues to this day to host international peace festivals.

The modern peace movement beyond New Zealand began prior to the Great War with voices supporting international arbitration between nations. Peace organisations such as the international women's movement lobbied until the eve of the outbreak of the Great War, as did the National Peace and Anti-Militarist League in New Zealand, which had long opposed conscription and compulsory military training. After the war autobiographies began appearing, of which perhaps the best known was Archibald Baxter's *We Will Not Cease*, which describes the dreadful treatment of New Zealand conscientious objectors during the war.[4]

These writings and others from overseas influenced anti-war sentiments, which continued to organise in support of peace after the Great War. Publications in the decade following the War reached New Zealand where they influenced the reading public, either as library borrowers or book buyers. Erich Maria Remarque's *All Quiet on the Western Front* was published in English in 1929 and was soon produced as a film, which played to packed New Zealand cinemas in 1931. Other notable titles included Robert Graves's *Goodbye to All That*, Richard Aldington's *Death of a Hero*, and A *Farewell to Arms* by Ernest Hemingway; a film of the latter was released one year after *All Quiet on the Western Front*, and was just as successful. While some of these works were presented as fiction, all contained autobiographical content. These works either openly projected an anti-war stance or, by describing the futility, brutality and sheer carnage of industrialised warfare, served the same end, even if this was not intended. A title first published in 1933, *Testament of Youth* by Vera Brittain, was influential in its day and continues to provide a powerful anti-war message to our generation through its film production in 2015.[5] Robin Hyde published *Passport to Hell* in 1936,[6] followed two years later by *Nor the Years Condemn*, based on her interviews with a former soldier. Hyde would later be recognised as an important New Zealand litterateur. These titles are but a small number taken from the canon of writings about the Great War, which also included some very influential war poetry.

Onto this stage of world events would come a new challenge to those seeking to restrain humankind from repeating the mistakes of the past: the Spanish Civil War. This was destined to cause a foreign policy rift between Britain and its Dominion in the South Pacific, when the New Zealand government voted to support the collective security policy of the League of Nations, in opposition to the policy of the United Kingdom.

This is the milieu in which the life and work of our subject will be examined. In so doing we grasp the idea that, as Ralph Waldo Emerson wrote, "There is no history: There is only Biography ... [each] individual must work out the whole problem of science, letters, and theology for himself, can owe his fathers nothing. There is no history; only biography."[7] While Emerson may have had an excessive regard for self-reliance, he still provides us with a valuable insight. Whereas the biographer may use the same methodologies as in other branches of history, biography uses the prism of one individual's life to provide a particular view of history. Biography seeks to understand a person's role within the larger historical process, as well as how they were shaped

Introduction

and influenced by that process; it also uses the individual life story to illuminate important events during the period in which they lived.

Literature about Norman Murray Bell

Very little has been published about Norman Murray Bell besides newspaper reports of school and university prizes which he won, and the story of his family origin (his grandparents came out to New Zealand as Albertland settlers). His name appears in official records, one of the earliest being the Thirty-third Annual Report of the Minister of Education to the New Zealand Parliament in 1910 recording the election of the first Trinity College, University of Cambridge scholar from this University: "and the choice fell upon Norman Murray Bell, MA., who proceeded to Cambridge to take up his duties in Michaelmas Term, 1909."[8]

Next, we find an account of Bell's academic prowess in the first history of Canterbury University College,[9] published after World War I, which summarises his record: winning a junior university scholarship, further scholarships in Greek and Physics, a BA in Greek and Chemistry, and an MA with First Class Honours in Classics and Chemistry. In Britain he was a Cambridge University BA with First Class Honours in Classics; a research student in Chemistry at Liverpool University; an external student at London University, where he completed a BD with First Class Honours in Theology; a research student in Chemistry and Education at St Andrews University, where he was the medallist in education. He attended the University of Bern in Switzerland, where he studied Philosophy of Science. The account records that after his return to New Zealand during the war, Bell refused to comply with the Military Service Act, was court-martialled and imprisoned. It goes on to say that "since 1919, [he was a] Private Tutor, being debarred from teaching in Government Schools."

The next official record of the University of Canterbury was the official *History of the University of Canterbury*, published in 1973.[10] (The University of New Zealand colleges had become independent universities in 1962.) It is remarkable for what it does not say: it does not refer to Norman Murray Bell, despite his status as one of the institution's most illustrious sons. Francis Haslam (1848-1924), the Professor of Classics who arranged for the Trinity College scholarship that Bell received, is recognised in the history as one of the first generation of scholars at Canterbury: "F. W. C. Haslam was the representative of a Cambridge tradition which placed the gentlemanly pursuit of style and elegance among the chief aims of university study."[11] However, the volume is silent about Haslam's efforts which created the Trinity College scholarship or the activities of its first recipient, Norman Murray Bell. It is strange, to say the very least, that this significant scholar should be written out of the university's history. Was this merely an oversight?[12]

The lacuna in the record spans another forty years before we next find mention of Norman Murray Bell, in a meticulously researched and recently published history of the vegetarian movement in New Zealand.[13] Norman Murray Bell exemplifies the intriguing connection that so often can be found between dedicated pacifists and the vegetarian and animal welfare belief systems. This connection echoes the ethics promoted by Albert Schweitzer (1875-1965) in his many writings on philosophy, theology and ethics, over a century ago. Schweitzer wrote:

> Slowly in our European thought comes the notion that ethics has not only to do with mankind but with the animal creation as well. This begins with St Francis of Assisi. The explanation which applies only to man must be given up. Thus we shall arrive at saying that ethics is reverence for *all* life. (Emphasis in the original.)

And elsewhere he wrote that human ethics consisted of a special responsibility:

> Ethics consist in responsibility towards all that lives — responsibility which has become so wide as to be limitless. Action directed towards the world is only possible for man in so far as he strives for the maintenance and furtherance at its highest level of all life that comes within his range. In this becoming-one with all life he realizes the active becoming-one with the Primal Source of Being to which all life belongs.[14]

In Bell's case, it took a "road to Damascus" type of experience for him to realise how the web of life was interconnected and sacred. This important psychological event, which Bell was to chronicle[15] and from which he gained important insight, resulted in his activities expanding from pacifism to include vegetarianism and animal welfare, causes which he continued to support until his death. In fact, his activities continued after his death, as he bequeathed funds to pay for advertisements promoting animal rights for the next thirty years.

Introduction

Some Issues to Be Examined

What were the ethical impulses that inspired Norman Murray Bell and others like him to strive for a better world? This is one of the questions that will be examined as we undertake his story, the classic story of a prophet without recognition in his own country. What emerges is a nexus between the political and the religious: two aspects of one person, opposite sides of the same coin.

In seeking to understand the sources of Norman Murray Bell's ethical positions, the first task is to understand what formed his view of society. What created his mental framework that served him so well during his lifetime? Can we identify influences in his intellectual development that stayed with him throughout his life, and that help make sense of the ethical positions he later adopted?

Secondly, we can trace the development of his religious thought from more orthodox religious positions to unorthodox belief, exploring the theological ideas that attracted him and the ethical concerns that influenced him. If there is any truth to the idea that war has a way of distorting religious principles, we may suspect that the major Christian churches' support of the Great War could have been a factor in his belief transformation.

Thirdly, clearly, there was an interaction between religion and politics throughout the adult life of Norman Murray Bell. It is the contention of this book that his moral impulses originated in his belief system, and that this was the motivating factor in his life story. However, it is not clear cut, as he also continued with religious advocacy. This may have been, in part, the result of the loss of civil rights after his release from prison, which limited his ability to find political expression for his beliefs.

Finally, there is the question of how well he succeeded in attaining his goals. To what extent was he able to work with and motivate others, to what extent did his personality isolate him and possibly limit the effectiveness of the work he was doing?

An Outline of the Life of Norman Murray Bell

The structure of this book follows a broad chronological pattern that allows for the examination and telling of Norman Murray Bell's life story within major themes.

Introduction

The first chapter, his early life in New Zealand from 1887 to 1909, discusses his family origins, beginning with the arrival of his grandparents, Dr James Bell (1836-1870) and Henrietta Mary Bell (1839-1913) from Devon in 1862. His grandfather was physician to the eight hundred nonconformist settlers who came to establish the colony of Albertland, sixty miles north of Auckland overlooking the Kaipara harbour. Intended to be the third religiously-based settlement following in the footsteps of Anglican Christchurch and Presbyterian Dunedin, this would be the last organised settlement in New Zealand. The Albertlanders were seeking freedom from the religious and social strictures of Victorian England. The settlement did not live up to its high hopes and for many turned into an economic failure; Norman Murray Bell's father, Horace Roland Bell (1863-1945), left the family home at Port Albert and went to Auckland where he found a career in the New Zealand Railways. In 1886 Horace married Annie McQuirk (née Coffey, 1863-1935) and their first child, Norman Murray Bell, was born on 28 January 1887.

Norman Murray Bell grew up in a conventional middle-class family. Under the New Zealand Education Act of 1877, all primary schooling was free, secular and compulsory. Norman began school in Parnell, Auckland. His father received a promotion in his work and was transferred, together with the family, finally reaching Lyttelton, the port for Christchurch City. This was to prove momentous for the young Norman Murray Bell, as his academic achievements led to a scholarship at Christ's College, which he attended from 1900 to 1904, becoming Head of School (equivalent to Dux, a term not used at Christ's College). This was a college which thought of itself following in the finest traditions of the English public schools. There he was confirmed into the Anglican Church and trained in the army cadets. Christ's College promoted a military ethos with the ideals of honour and duty, preparing pupils for the eventuality that the British Empire might require their services. Patriotism in military form was the expectation. On leaving school in 1904, Bell won a university scholarship and several university prizes, which enabled him to attend Canterbury University College for the next five years. He graduated from the University of New Zealand with a BA and MA in classics and chemistry in 1909. His academic career in

Introduction

New Zealand culminated in an award that would take him to Trinity College, Cambridge University.

Chapter 2 examines Norman Murray Bell's intellectual development at universities in Britain and the Continent, from 1909 to 1916. In this stage of his life he was a young man on a great intellectual adventure. Life at Trinity College from 1909 to 1912 was exhilarating: he completed his BA with first-class honours and won the College Classics prize. His Tutor was a Fellow of Trinity College, William Whetham, who undertook work in experimental physics at the Cavendish Laboratory and later wrote about the dangers of "race deterioration;"[16] his views on social Darwinism were such as Sir Francis Galton, Honorary Fellow of the College, would no doubt have approved. Other notable Fellows at this time whose names would live on in history included the Honourable Bertrand Russell, Lecturer in Logic and the Principles of Mathematics; George Macaulay Trevelyan, who was Lecturer in History; and John Maynard Keynes, Director of Studies in Economics.[17] This was a time when the Apostles, a Cambridge conversazione society whose membership amongst select undergraduates was secret, provided intellectual stimulation to its members. Several of the Trinity College Fellows and undergraduates were members of the Apostles and had significant cross-fertilization with the Bloomsbury Group, an Edwardian circle of artists and writers who adopted liberal ideas, including pacifism, while challenging many Victorian conventions. Although Norman Murray Bell may never have had been directly involved with these groups, he would have "rubbed shoulders" with some of their members and become familiar with their ideas. He would have stood out amongst his peers, being older than most undergraduates, a colonial and an outstanding classicist.

Bell next appears to have followed two academic pursuits concurrently. He enrolled for a bachelor of divinity degree at the University of London in 1912 as an external student, completing it with an honours paper in Theology in 1915. He was in residence as a visiting researcher in the Chemistry Department at the University of Liverpool for two years between 1913 and 1914,[18] and subsequently jointly published experimental reports in a Royal Society of Chemistry Journal and authored a scientific report in another journal. He went on to St Andrews University, at Fife in Scotland, as a research student in Education, and was awarded the Education medal. He spent one academic year at St

Andrews, 1914-1915, of a planned two-year prelude to taking a DPhil there. Then he spent time on the continent, studying Philosophy of Science for one year at Bern University in Switzerland, 1915-1916. There are reports that he attended Heidelberg University in Germany, where he could only have audited courses, as there is no record of his matriculation or formal enrolment. The problem with this claim, which is not supported by any evidence, is that war had broken out; as a British subject he was unlikely to gain admission into the country, let alone study at a German university.

During the time he was studying and travelling on the Continent, Bell was also completing his theology study at London University. It is most likely that he developed his ideas about pacifism, which he saw as intricately linked to his Christian belief, either during his Bachelor of Divinity studies or around the time he returned from Bern. Just how this came about is one of the important issues to look at. He may have come into contact with the Theistic Church, then led by the Rev. Walter Walsh (1857-1931), which opposed war and advocated pacifism. This has significance for the later evolution of his religious ideas expressed in the Free Religious Movement.

Chapter 3 focuses on Bell's experiences during and immediately after the war. In the year before his return to New Zealand, while his family no doubt basked in the justifiable pride of their elder son's successes, Norman Murray Bell was portrayed as a scholar at war. The hubris and jingoism surrounding the war created this false expectation. The press in New Zealand learned about his chemistry work and created a story that it was war-related and soon to be crowned with an army commission. To make matters worse, the story was linked to the bravery of his brother Harold (1891-1958), then serving in the New Zealand Army and wounded in the Gallipoli campaign.

Upon his return to New Zealand, Bell, now twenty-nine years old, obtained a temporary full-time appointment as assistant master and demonstrator in physics at Christchurch Boys High School from 1 March 1917.[19] His tenure as a teacher would be short-lived, however. As a pacifist, he knew he would soon run up against the requirements of the Military Service Act 1916, which required the registration of all non-Māori men between the ages of 20 to 46 years. (Although the Act had a very narrow provision for religious objection, Bell did not

Introduction

avail himself of an application on these grounds. He would have been unlikely to succeed had he done so; only thirty exemptions at most were granted during the war.) Publicly known to be a religious objector, Bell was arrested on 28 August 1917 for breach of the Act and sent to a military camp. At Trentham Military Camp, following 28 days detention for refusing a medical examination, he was convicted at a district court-martial of disobeying lawful commands given by a superior officer and sentenced to two years imprisonment with hard labour.[20]

Following his release from prison, his political ambitions were thwarted by legal restrictions which deprived conscientious objectors of their civil rights. In some way, this served to intensify the nexus between his religious outlook and his political activism. We find Bell working in 1919 on behalf of the Conscientious Objectors' Fellowship, struggling for the freedom of those still imprisoned after peace had been declared because their sentence was not fully served. Prohibited from any government-related work, such as a university college teacher, he supported himself as a private instructor for secondary students and a part-time Tutor in sociology for the Workers' Educational Association.

Chapter 4 largely covers the interbellum period in New Zealand: pacifism, politics and religion, between 1921 and 1939. Contemporaneously with his religious work, Bell was campaigning throughout the 1920s and 30s on the political front: by 1934 he was national president of the No More War campaign, which functioned in tandem with the Free Religious Movement. He also began working with the Rev. James Chapple (1865-1947). Chapple had been convicted of sedition in 1918 and sentenced to 11 months imprisonment for speaking out against the war. Bell and Chapple may have known each other from the common experience of having been imprisoned at the same time. Chapple followed in the established tradition of radical religion in Christchurch, which was never far from radical politics: a heritage that began with Our Father's Church, founded by the Rev. James O'Bryan Hoare (1835-1914) in 1894 and the Socialist (Labour) Church, established by Harry Atkinson (1867-1956) in 1896. Both had run their course by 1917, when Chapple became minister to the Unitarian Progressive Society. When Chapple retired Bell took over leadership, transforming the organisation into the Free Religious Movement. When Chapple retired Bell took over leadership, transforming the organisation into the Free Religious Movement.

In 1930 Bell experienced a unique psychological event, one that was to transform his life. Typically for a man of his intellect, he chronicled what happened. In a period of altered consciousness, he saw the web of life that connected all living things. This revelation intensified and expanded his religious outlook, becoming a unified faith and gospel. He embraced the creed of vegetarianism and expounded it with unsurpassed zeal. Not that he dropped any of his peace activities; he continued working with the National Peace Council, No More War Movement and the Movement Against War and Fascism.

The final chapter covers World War II and Bell's later life and legacy. As in the first World War, support for pacifism diminished as legal strictures were enacted which suppressed public advocacy of peace or criticism of the government war effort. During the war he struggled to publish the pacifist journal *Cosmos*, printing it by hand and delivering copies on foot. His home was often raided by the police, at the instigation of the security authorities searching for evidence of any seditious activities. The aftermath of the war found Bell a lonely figure continuing to deliver a pacifist voice in society. At the war's end, he was living in the old family home with one of his sisters who, like him, had remained unmarried; both of their parents had died. After the war, he could be found with a chair and small table sitting in Cathedral Square, the heart of Christchurch, with his petition calling for people to sign up opposing all war, but especially nuclear war, and seeking support for animal welfare.

Bell decided to apply to have his Cambridge University MA conferred, as he was entitled to do being a BA graduate, and this was done in absentia in 1949. He found relaxation translating the Bible from Hebrew and had completed translating the Book of Genesis not long before his death. He continued with his peace and vegetarian advocacy. But his journey did not quite end with his death in 1962. Having provided in his will that his estate be spent on monthly advertisements in two Christchurch newspapers for the next thirty years, he ensured that he would speak beyond his age and time, calling for peace between humans and domesticated animals.

First Albertlanders leave for New Zealand

Farewell to Matilda Wattenbach

1

A Dissenting Heritage and the Challenge of Orthodoxy

Albertland, Auckland and Christchurch, 1862-1909

When the *Matilda Wattenbach* sailed into Auckland Harbour on 8 September 1862 it was the first of the ships that would comprise the last organised settlement in New Zealand, and one uniquely consisting of some 2,000 members from nonconformist churches in England.[1] They sought to emulate earlier successful settlements with a religious character: Anglicans in Christchurch and Presbyterians in Dunedin. Included amongst them were Baptists, Presbyterians, Congregationalists, Wesleyans, Independents, Quakers and Unitarians. Non-Subscribing Presbyterians from Ireland and the occasional Anglican family could be found amongst the settlers. The *Wattenbach* left Gravesend, the first port on the River Thames, accompanied by the *Hanover*. They were given a rousing farewell by about 15,000 people gathered on the London docks, listening to speeches and singing hymns accompanied by a brass band.[2]

Some of the settlers destined for New Zealand at this time might otherwise have headed for the United States of America, which had been in the grip of civil war since 1861. Unfortunately, New Zealand's civil war had broken out at the same time. Compared to that in America, however, it was viewed in a very different light in Victorian England, where it was seen as a rebellion by some Māori tribes against the colonial government. At the heart of the rebellion was the transfer of

Chapter 1

Māori land to the government and thus eventual settler ownership. This conflict would become known as the Land Wars and major campaigns continued into 1866.

Included in the cabin class passengers of the *Matilda Wattenbach* (as opposed to steerage class, which was standard for most of the passengers) was the organiser of the Albertland Settlement Scheme, the Rev. William Rawson Brame (1832-1863), a Baptist minister from Birmingham. Also travelling cabin class was the minister to the settlers, the Rev. Samuel Edger (1823-1882), his wife Louisa and four children, and the physician Dr James Bell (1836-1870) and his wife Henrietta (1839-1913). All of them would play important roles in the settlement.[3] Brame had formed an association to promote a nonconformist settlement in New Zealand, capitalised in part on the sentiment aroused from the bi-centenary of the expulsion of nonconforming ministers from the Church of England. By the time the first ships sailed, a Board of Management had been formed, with Brame as President, Dr James Bell as Vice-President and Treasurer, and the Rev. Samuel Edger appointed to care for the religious needs of the settlers. His vision was of a non-sectarian Christian Church that would unite all the settlers in a common bond of fellowship and service. A community formed on co-operative Christian principles was envisioned, based on religious freedom of

Rev. William Rawson Brame

Rev. Samuel Edger

thought and without the social strictures that pervaded English class society. A Co-operative Agricultural Implement Association was formed to purchase implements and tools for hire to the settlers, to save the expense of each settler providing for himself separately.

Insofar as the settlers believed in complete equality amongst religious beliefs without an established church, these expectations for the new colony were well founded. The issue had arisen nearly twenty years previously at a meeting of the Legislative Council, the body which governed New Zealand with the Governor during the Crown Colony period.

The Imperial government in London had funded the Rev. Dr George Selwyn (1809-1878), the first Anglican Bishop to the colony, and in 1844 the colonial government was asked to pay for an increase to cover his travel expenses. When the issue came before the Legislative Council in June that year, Dr Samuel Martin (c.1805-1848) presented a petition from the Auckland settlers calling for the ecclesiastical item to be struck out of the estimates. This was the opening shot in a fight between Governor Robert Fitzroy (1805-1865), who supported the funding proposal, and the egalitarian-minded Scottish Highlander, Samuel McDonald Martin, a graduate of the University of Glasgow with an MD in 1835. He was appointed a magistrate for New Zealand in 1841 and took up editorship of the *New Zealand Herald and Auckland Gazette* in 1842. He became editor of the *Southern Cross* in 1843 and continued to expose corrupt land deals and inept practices in the administration. Fitzroy approved of his cogent editorial style and had appointed him to the Legislative Council in May 1844. Dr Martin made a forceful speech for the separation of church and state, opposing the Governor and moving that nothing be provided for by way of ecclesiastical establishments:

> He objected on principle to any attempt at setting up a state church in this colony. The evils arising from the connection between church and state in the mother country were so great and so manifest, that he hoped the members of this Council would at once oppose this first step towards laying the foundation of a state church ...
>
> [He opposed the motion because] it would have the effect creating religious controversies and quarrels, which would be most injurious in any country, but more especially in a new colony like this. Every sect should be allowed to support their own clergymen, and no man should

be compelled to pay towards the maintenance of a religion which he did not in his conscience believe to be true ... believing that every man had a right to think for himself, and that mind was free and unfettered ... he disapproved of the attempt to establish the supremacy of any one church over the others in this colony.[4]

When the vote was taken the Governor's proposal was lost by five votes to two. Within a few years, settler representation in government would dramatically improve with the introduction of the New Zealand Constitution Act 1852. This Act established a bicameral legislature: the Legislative Council was re-established as an Upper House to which members were appointed, while the House of Representatives was the lower house with elected members. Six provinces were founded, each with an elected Provincial Council. So far as the Albertland settlement was concerned, the Auckland Provincial Government authorised a freehold land grant of 40 acres for each man plus a further 40 acres for his wife and 20 acres for each child aged between 5 and 18 years, provided they stayed on the land for at least five years.[5] This land was situated on an arm of the Kaipara Harbour, comprising 60,000 acres at Oruawharo. Much of the land around the harbour was covered with stands of kauri trees, which would prove invaluable for the settlers, providing timber for building or sale. The shoreline was known as the Kauri Coast.

Vessels loading timber at Port Albert

By the time the Albertland ships started arriving, hostilities between Māori and Europeans had broken out in the Waikato, south of Auckland, causing fear amongst the settlers that war could spread to Auckland and reach the Kaipara area. All the Kaipara chiefs, including Arama Karaka and Paikea Te Hekeua, who had converted to Christianity, wrote reassuringly in the *Albertland Gazette* about their friendship for the settlers, saying they wished "to live at peace with all men" and expressing their "determination is to keep this trouble far from the people of Kaipara."[6] Indeed, without the regular help of local Māori, life for the Albertlanders would have been harder than it was.

Dr James Bell, Pioneer Doctor at Port Albert

The Albertland medical practitioner had been invited to a meeting with the Kaipara Māori chiefs to discuss the possible threat to the settlers. The most obvious danger was from the war in the south, as it crept closer to Auckland, but what if the tribes north of the Kaipara should opportunistically join in the rebellion? Dr Bell came away from his meeting reassured that local Māori would act to protect the settlers if necessary, by collecting them from their outlying farms and bringing them to Port Albert, where the settlers could defend themselves en masse should they be threatened. The local chiefs recommended that the only preparation settlers take was to ensure they were adequately armed.[7] In the event, the Albertland settlers were not threatened with the war that raged for a time well south of the Kaipara, deep in the Waikato and Taranaki regions.

Meanwhile of the three leading lights of the settlement movement who had sailed out together, William Brame died within a year of his arrival. Samuel Edger established a non-sectarian church that found favour with many settlers, until after six years at Port Albert his residence was consumed by fire "during the morning service of Sunday, August 8th, 1866",[8] destroying nearly every book he had. As a result of this loss, Rev. Edger moved to Auckland, becoming a non-denominational preacher in that town.

Dr Bell, described as "the fine big Scot",[9] settled in the hills above Port Albert, about two miles from where the new town was planned. He had qualified at Edinburgh with a Licentiate of the Royal College

Chapter 1

Dr James Bell and Mrs Henrietta Bell

of Surgeons in 1857 and a Licentiate of the Royal College of Physicians in 1860.[10] At the time he decided to emigrate with his wife Henrietta Mary (née Turton, originally from Burton upon Trent in Staffordshire), he was listed on the United Kingdom Medical Register as practising at Broad Clyst, near Exeter in Devon. The couple had married in 1859 in Amoy, China (the Europeanised version of Xiamen), a provincial city in Fujian beside the Taiwan Strait.[11] It was a centre for missionary work, having well established Dutch Reformed and London Missionary Society churches. The Presbyterian Church Foreign Missions Committee was also active in this area. After completing their missionary work the newly married couple left China in 1860.

James Bell was appointed Coroner for the Kaipara region on 29 December 1862.[12] On 27 June 1868 he registered under the Medical Practitioners Act 1867, the first statute to regulate the medical profession in New Zealand.

In addition to developing a farm on the allocated land, Dr Bell purchased additional land, giving a total of 248 acres (about 100 hectares). As the only medical practitioner in the area he faced considerable demand for his services. Fortunately, he found a competent obstetric

A Dissenting Heritage and the Challenge of Orthodoxy

Sarah Jerome Becroft

nurse who had come out on the same ship. Sarah Jerome (née Morris, 1812-1870) had married Joseph Jerome, an artist and painter, at the Wesleyan Chapel at Newport, Isle of Wight, on 16 July 1843. Now widowed, Mrs Jerome was travelling on the *Matilda Wattenbach* with her teenage son and daughter when she met John Becroft (1814-1892), a widower with his six sons and three daughters. During the voyage, Mrs Jerome helped care for one of his daughters who became ill. "Mrs Jerome nursed the child with all her considerable skill. In spite of all that she could do, the girl died, but a strong link had been formed between John and Sarah."[13] John Becroft and Sarah Jerome were married upon their arrival in Auckland in September 1862. Mrs Becroft became Dr Bell's chief assistant and her services as nurse and midwife were often called upon. Frequently having to walk long distances to her patients, it is recorded that she was "proud of her record of never having lost a maternity case."[14]

In August 1870, while visiting a patient at Wharehine, an area adjoining Albertland, Dr Bell became ill. A dramatic attempt was made to save the doctor: "Mr Harden was sent off post-haste to the

Chapter 1

Doctor's home some two miles up the Oruawharo [river] ... to bring back the required medicine." Mr Harden was obviously travelling by boat as "An adverse tide and strong headwind delayed Mr Harden by some hours. By the time he reached his home again, it was too late. Dr Bell was beyond help and did not survive long."[15] At the time it was said he died of appendicitis, so Dr Bell may have been planning to operate on himself, a not unheard-of event. However, his official death record gives peritonitis as the cause, indicating how far his condition had deteriorated.[16]

The esteem in which Dr Bell was held is shown in the public meeting of ratepayers of the local Highway District a few weeks after his death:

> By the death of Dr Bell this district has lost one of its best and most generous friends. He arrived in New Zealand with the first party of Albertland settlers, and was one of the first to settle on the land. His professional services were for the most part, from that day until recently, given freely to any and all who stood in need of them, over a wide tract of country from Te Arai to Northern Wairoa.[17]

The writer went to say that "Few indeed, if any, can estimate rightly" how this man with a naturally strong constitution could be undermined "by exposure to the wind, rain and storm."

In the vote that took place to fill the trustee vacancy arising from Dr Bell's death, John Becroft, husband of Dr Bell's nurse, was elected as one of the Highway trustees for the district.

Dr Bell was only thirty-four years old when he died, leaving his widow Henrietta with six small children to raise alone: three sons and three daughters ranging from a baby to a seven-year-old. This tragedy for Henrietta followed the loss of her mother Elizabeth Turton (1802-1867), who had joined them in New Zealand in 1865 and died at Port Albert two years later. Henrietta decided to return to England with Florence (1861-1946), Lucy (1867-1926), and the baby May (1870-1961).

When Henrietta decided to go to England she left the three boys in the care of relatives in Auckland. The eldest son was Horace Roland (1863-1945), the second Henry Norman (1868-1944) and the younger brother Harold (1869-1889). It seems likely that Harold went to England to work so he could be near his mother. He was working as an ordinary seaman on the sailing vessel *Killochan* when it collided with the steamship *Nereid* in the English Channel; both ships foundered within minutes and twenty-three lives were lost. Harold was only twenty years old when he drowned in February 1889.

Leaving Albertland: Auckland and Beyond

Henrietta Bell returned to New Zealand in 1882 after a twelve-year sojourn and remained a widow, living her last years at Mt Pleasant Hospital, near Dargaville.

In 1886 her daughter May Elizabeth Margaret Bell married William Tullibardine Murray at Lincoln Street, Ponsonby, the Rev. Thomas Spurgeon officiating. Rev. Spurgeon had arrived from London in 1881 where he had officiated at the Baptist Metropolitan Tabernacle. He accepted a similar position in Auckland and for a time was the travelling evangelist for the Baptist Union. Mr Murray was a school teacher when he married May, but later trained to be a minister and was ordained as a Home Missionary in the Presbyterian Church in 1917. He had ministries in Hanmer, a small town in Canterbury well known for its hot pools and nearby ski field; and Normanby, a small village in South Taranaki. While in Taranaki Murray climbed Mt Egmont in February 1923 and perished in a snowstorm. His body was never found.

A few months later, in March 1886, Horace Bell married Annie McQuirk Coffey (1863-1935), a recent arrival from Glasgow, at Lincoln Street in Ponsonby, where Horace was living with his uncle Harold James Bell while working for the New Zealand Railways. The wedding was conducted by the Rev. William Gittos (1830-1916). The Rev. Gittos had been the pioneer Wesleyan missionary to the Kaipara Māori. He had welcomed the first Albertland settlers from the *Matilda Wattenbach* and forged a great friendship with them. Now in failing health, retired and living nearby in Ponsonby, he was happy to officiate at the wedding.

In the New Year, Annie Bell gave birth to Norman Murray Bell, on 28 January 1887. (He would be the first of eight children, three boys and five girls.) The occupation of Horace Bell was given as Station Master and the family were living in Avondale, Auckland. From there Horace was sent to Huntly to the post of Station Master. When he was sent further south to Te Aroha in 1891, the residents of Huntly presented

Chapter 1

*Annie Bell with her three sons
(left to right) Norman, Wilfred and Harold
wearing Bell clan kilts c.1902*

him with a handsome testimonial in the form of a marble clock. By 1896 Horace was in charge of the Paeroa railway station some 21 kilometres away. While there he took Presbyterian Church services at the nearby schoolhouse. Annie took the opportunity to support the petition for women's suffrage, which succeeded in getting women the vote in 1893, making New Zealand the first country to do so. In 1896 the Minister of Railways transferred Horace back to Auckland to be a clerk in the District Traffic Manager's office — promotion at last![18] Now the family had a settled period in Auckland but it was only to last for a few years.

A Parliamentary Committee was set up in 1898 to consider the Wellington-Lyttelton steamer service.[19] The Minister of Railways was included because of the need to examine the train services in the colony. It heard how poorly services were coordinated from the various centres, resulting in inefficiency and delays. It was anticipated that a traveller should be able to leave Auckland on a Monday by steamer, arrive at Lyttelton in the South Island on Wednesday morning, then reach Dunedin via rail by Wednesday night. Efficiencies in freight deliveries were included in the committee's terms of reference. (The railway link between Auckland and Wellington had yet to be built; it would take another ten years to be completed.) When the Railways Department selected a person to manage the new transport hub, it fell to Horace Bell, who was transferred to Lyttelton, the port for Christchurch, the main city of the Canterbury Province.

The Bell Family in Canterbury: The Education of Norman Murray Bell

The transfer and promotion meant that Horace was now managing an important hub connecting rail and shipping services from the main centres of both Islands. By the time the Bell family moved to Lyttelton there were three children; Norman, his sister Winifred and younger brother Harold. The Bell family settled into the port village, which had been developing since the 1850s and was seen as an attractive place to live. Horace was handling the demands of a senior role within the Railways Department, integrating the commercial demands of South Island rail and shipping. Lyttelton was linked to Christchurch by rail, a tunnel through the Port Hills having been constructed in 1867. Later Horace and Annie would decide to move the family home to Christchurch.

Chapter 1

Christ's College, Christchurch

A Dissenting Heritage and the Challenge of Orthodoxy

The young Norman Murray Bell attended the West Lyttelton School and in his first year, 1898, won the Standard V class prize. The next year he was in Standard VI where he became Dux boy of the School and won a Christ's College scholarship. Norman Murray Bell was second, out of twenty-five candidates, in the Christ's College Entrance Scholarship examinations. The scholarships provided for two years of free education at the premier Anglican Boys College in the colony. How did this come about?

The Canterbury colony was born out of conservative Anglican reaction to Catholic emancipation in Ireland, as well as opposition to political liberalism and the spread of secular ideas. This was organised into the Oxford Movement, a high church form of Anglicanism led by conservative churchmen. The Oxford Movement's aims were promoted by the publication of Tracts, advocating the return to traditional liturgical practices and reintroduction of some Roman Catholic practices, which led to disputes about ritualism and subsequent court cases. One notable Tractarian, the Rev. John Keble (1792-1866), occupied a Chair of Poetry and had an Oxford College named after him. The Oxford Movement established religious orders and began working in the slums of London. From these ministries they developed a critique of British society out of which the Christian Social Union was established, demanding social justice for the poor and working classes.

A follower of the Rev. John Keble was the Anglo-Irish barrister John Godley (1814-1861) who was caught up in the Oxford Movement while a student at Christ Church College, Oxford. His wife Charlotte (née Griffith Wynne, 1821-1907) from Wales was inspired by the Evangelical wing of Anglicanism. Having seen the appalling famine in Ireland, Godley believed that large-scale immigration could be a solution. He discussed these ideas with Edward Gibbon Wakefield, who was involved in planning settlements in New Zealand. Godley, according to American historian David Hackett Fischer, was "no Democrat or Liberal ... He reacted very strongly against the principles of the American and French revolutions, and also against some of the values of the Enlightenment."[20] He established the Canterbury Association in 1848 based on the duties laid down by revealed religion. The

Chapter 1

River Avon, Christchurch

influences of ecclesiastical and political Anglicanism were paramount in his thinking. The Association members included two archbishops and seven bishops who were leaders in the Oxford Movement. The Association, which would become known as the Canterbury Pilgrims, aimed to build an Anglican utopia in New Zealand. It was planned to reflect an ideal English society, including Victorian class structure. To be accepted, each immigrant had to produce a letter from their vicar confirming they were sober, industrious and honest as well as being amongst the most respectable of their class.

John Godley named the main town Christchurch after his Oxford college. The Port of Lyttelton was named after Charlotte Godley's eminent brother-in-law Lord Lyttelton. When the first fleet of four ships arrived in 1850 they were greeted by the Godleys. Until his departure two years later John Godley was the de facto governor of the settlement. In 1852 under the New Zealand Constitution Act, the Province of Canterbury was created with an elected Provincial Council and Superintendent. Now was time for the Godleys to return to England.

One of the early laws passed by the new Provincial Council was an Ordinance for the foundation, endowment and maintenance of Christ's College, Canterbury. Under the Ecclesiastical and Educational Institutions of the Settlement, the College would propagate the Christian religion professed and taught by the United Church of England and Ireland.[21]

Norman Murray Bell attended Christ's College for five years, between the ages of 13 and 17 years. He would have been a boarder at Christ's College, given that the family were living at Lyttelton. During the first two years his father would have had to meet the costs of about £14 per term for junior boys boarding in one of the School Houses, a not inconsiderable amount in those days. (Norman's Entrance Scholarship only covered the costs of tuition.)

Norman Murray Bell began student life in 1900 in a Special Form between the Lower and Upper Fourth Form. He came first in Latin, English and French, receiving the class prizes for those subjects. In 1901 he was in a Remove Form between the Upper Fourth and Lower Fifth Forms. In both these years, the forms were divided into two divisions and in both years Bell was in the first division. For his 1901 year, he was first in Latin, French and Mathematics, winning the Class Prize in those subjects. In addition, he achieved a further scholarship and a special exhibition; these achievements would have paid his tuition costs and boarding expenses for the following years. In 1902 he was in the Upper Fifth form where he was first in Latin, English, French, Science and Mathematics, receiving the Class Prize in those subjects, besides receiving the Tancred Prizes in History and Literature. These latter two prizes are awarded on the results of elective examinations in each subject.

In the Lower Sixth Form in 1903 Bell won the form prizes in Latin, French and Science in addition to the Tancred Prizes in History and Literature. This year he was also the recipient of the Balfour Divinity Prize for being first in that class. He was successful in achieving a further Entrance Scholarship and a Board of Education Senior Scholarship. In 1904, his final year, Bell was in the Upper Sixth Form. There he won the form prizes in Latin, French, Science and English, and once again the Tancred Prizes in History and Literature and the Balfour Prize in Divinity. He also received a Board of Education Senior Scholarship.

For many of the scholarships and exhibitions that he won it was a requirement that the applicant must be a member of the Church of England or a church in communion with it. There were morning services

Chapter 1

at the Chapel on all weekdays and Saturday, with special services on Holy days. All boys were prepared for confirmation by the Chaplain and there was an annual confirmation service conducted by the Warden, who for the time being was the Lord Bishop of Christchurch.[22] From this, we can conclude that Norman Murray Bell became a member of the Church of England.

The Sub-Warden of the College was the Rev. Harper, Dean of Christchurch. He spelt out the ethos of the College on a Commemoration Day Annual Address when he said that: "... the one great ideal of the founders of the College — that it should resemble as closely as possible, those grand institutions, the public schools of England — had been always kept in view."[23] At the same Commemoration Day observances, tribute was paid to Major Richards, who had a 21-year connection with the school, having established the Cadet Corps in 1881. It is noteworthy that from 1864 to 1902 the introduction of military training, following the tradition of British Public Schools, was entirely controlled by the Headmaster; the Army was not formally involved. The Education Act of 1902 was responsible for the formation of cadet units in New Zealand secondary schools and the Army involvement in their training. This was a consequence of the South African Wars. However, military drill and participation in the Cadet Corps at Christ's College had been compulsory for all boys, unless specially exempted by the Headmaster, for more than twenty years before legal authority created this requirement. Therefore, in the absence of any evidence to the contrary, we must assume Norman Murray Bell received military training at school along with his fellow students.

In his final year, the results for the examinations sat in the previous year were published and Norman Murray Bell obtained a credit pass in the University of New Zealand Junior Scholarship. He was also Head of School in 1904, which means he was Academic Head of School. Christ's College does not use the term Dux, a term typically used to refer to the highest academically ranked student.

The year after he left Christ's College, the results for the Junior Scholarship examination sat in December 1904 were known and Norman Murray Bell was placed third nationally. His old school was so delighted that a half-day holiday was declared in honour of his success. The College celebrated by watching the cricket match between Canterbury and Australia,[24] not entirely an unexpected choice as the College made known that cricket was the chief school game. However, a search of the *Christ's College Registers,* published three times a year during Norman Murray Bell's time as a student, fails to mention him as having any sporting prowess at all. There was, therefore, a certain incongruity in the way his achievement was celebrated. The match was played at Lancaster Park and the touring Australians, who came from Melbourne, finally won comfortably by an innings and 108 runs.

Entering Canterbury University College on 4 March 1905, as a University Scholarship holder with an established academic career at one of the country's leading schools, Norman Murray Bell was well positioned to succeed. Enrolling for a BA, in 1906 he won Exhibitions in Greek and Chemistry. In 1907 he received the Sir George Grey Scholarship awarded to the first ranked scholar. It provided funds which would be sufficient for one or two year's sustenance. That year he also won Exhibitions in Greek and Physics.

Norman Murray Bell graduated with a BA in 1908 and senior scholarships in Greek and Chemistry. Although he did not study Greek at school, he became an outstanding scholar in the subject at university. In 1909 he graduated from the University of New Zealand with an MA, with First Class Honours in Classics and Second Class Honours in Chemistry.[25] In that same year he was nominated by the Board of Governors of Canterbury College for the first exhibition scholarship offered to study at Trinity College, Cambridge. The scholarship was for three years for the study of classics. Upon receiving the Trinity College scholarship, Bell resigned the government research scholarship awarded to him in chemistry. He had been engaged in research work dealing particularly with the evolution of oxygen from bleaching powder solutions under the influence of small quantities of cobalt salts and the modification of that again by various chemical compounds.[26]

When a large gathering of staff and students of Canterbury College met to bid Norman Murray Bell farewell in September 1909, he was described as having "a most brilliant scholastic career … [He] is an Auckland boy, being a grandson of the late Dr James Bell, of Port Albert. He began his schooling in Parnell before his family shifted to Lyttelton."[27]

Chapter 1

Even after all his years in Canterbury his Albertland heritage was remembered. In the following year, the Report of the Minister of Education to the New Zealand Parliament in 1910 recording the election of the first Trinity College, University of Cambridge scholar from this University: "and the choice fell upon Norman Murray Bell, M.A., who proceeded to Cambridge to take up his duties in Michaelmas Term, 1909."[28]

2

Intellectual Development
University Life and Religious Study in Britain and the Continent, 1909-1916

University of Cambridge, 1909-1912

Norman Murray Bell departed New Zealand in August 1909 on board the SS *Athenic*, the first of three identical ships of the White Star line built for the passenger and freight service between London and Wellington early in the twentieth century. He arrived at Cambridge in time for the Michaelmas term, which started on 1st October 1909. *The Cambridge University Calendars* for 1910-11 and 1912-13 described him as the New Zealand Exhibitor, Dominus N. M. Bell.[1] (As an academical title "Dominus" was used for graduates and in English colloquial use became "don" for fellows or tutors.) He also held a New Zealand government scholarship of £100 per year for three years towards his BA studies. His enrolment entry in 1909 lists him as a Sub-Sizar, as he received a small grant. According to the *Calendar* about 20 Sub-Sizars were admitted each year, the value of the Sub-Sizarship being £35 a year and was tenable with an Exhibition, so would have been a welcome addition toward Norman Murray Bell's living expenses.

In 1910 the *Transactions and Proceedings of the Royal Society of New Zealand* published a scientific paper by Norman Murray Bell.[2] This, together with his older than average age and graduate status, would have made the colonial student stand out among the other BA students, some 76 in number, attending Trinity College. His Tutor, William Cecil Dampier Whetham, MA, FRS (1867-1952), was a scientist who

Chapter 2

Norman Murray Bell and friend, London, 1910

Intellectual Development

Francis Haslam   *William Whetham*

undertook research at the Cavendish Laboratory (Physics Department), which earned him a Trinity College Fellowship in 1891. He became a Fellow of the Royal Society in 1901 when he was a lecturer in physics at Trinity College, where he wrote several books about the physical sciences. Though the College would have been aware that Professor Haslam, who had arranged the scholarship, was a classicist and Norman Murray Bell had a double major, William Whetham was his appointed Tutor, which would have been very beneficial if Bell had continued with his studies in chemistry.

William Whetham had already worked with an outstanding New Zealand scholar and knew that the small Pacific colony could send its brightest students. The first New Zealand scholar and researcher from outside Cambridge to receive a place at the Cavendish Laboratory, Ernest Rutherford (1871-1931), had also worked with William Whetham. After graduating from Canterbury University College with an MA in physical sciences and mathematics and BSc in geology and chemistry in 1895, Ernest Rutherford initially looked to a teaching career at Christchurch Boys High School. Fortunately, as it turned

Chapter 2

Ernest Rutherford

Charles Chilton

out for his career, he soon returned to university research and was awarded an Exhibition of 1851 scholarship, after it had been declined by the first candidate. He used this award to study at the Cavendish Laboratory between 1895 and 1898. Rutherford was one of the first to be awarded the new Cambridge BA research degree in 1897. During his time at Cambridge, he advocated equal privileges for women and men students, perhaps showing the influence of his fiancée's mother, a staunch suffragette in New Zealand. In 1901 he received his DSc degree from the University of New Zealand. In 1908, the year before Norman Murray Bell arrived at Cambridge, while professor of physics at Manchester, Rutherford was awarded the Nobel Prize in chemistry.[3]

Norman Murray Bell enrolled for a BA in Classics; normally the classical Tripos took three years of study, but given his qualifications from the University of New Zealand Bell was able to complete his degree in two years. He gained a first-class pass (division 2) and was awarded the College classics prize in 1912. During the long summer university holidays in 1910 Bell went to the Lake District, a mountainous region in Cumbria in northwest England, famous for its lakes

Intellectual Development

John Maynard Keynes *Bertrand Russell*

and forests and its association with the "Lake Poets" Wordsworth, Coleridge and Southey. He found a cottage to stay in with friends. It was part of a tour that Bell enjoyed for several weeks. His first holiday since he arrived in Britain was indicative of his ability to organise travel by train, bus or bicycle. He also visited London, taking time to explore the city, including having his photo taken with a friend in a studio on the Strand, not far from Covent Garden, where they may have taken in some live theatre.

Professor Charles Chilton (1860-1929), who had the chair in biology at Canterbury University College, and Mrs Chilton, visited some British universities during 1912, including Manchester, where they met Ernest Rutherford, and Cambridge, where they met Norman Murray Bell.

There were many prominent people on the staff at Trinity College while Bell was there, and some who would soon become even more well-known. The Director of Studies in Economics, John Maynard Keynes (1883-1946), produced outstanding work at the end of the Great War and later the Great Depression, and wrote his prescient

Chapter 2

work *The Economic Consequences of the Peace* when he saw the inherent danger emerging at the Versailles settlements. The Lecturer in Logic and Mathematics, the Hon. Bertrand Arthur William Russell (1872-1970), was already well known. Both Keynes and Russell had been members of the Cambridge Apostles (so nicknamed because the Cambridge Conversazione Society, its correct title, was formed by twelve evangelical students in 1820). During the time Norman Murray Bell was at Cambridge, other members who attended the society's weekly meetings included the philosopher G. E. Moore (1873-1958), whose work, including *Principia Ethica* (1903), was very influential amongst fellow Apostles; the novelist E. M. Foster (1879-1970), two of whose most well-known books, *Howards End* and *A Room With a View*, were published by 1910; the biographer Lytton Strachey (1880-1932), who wrote *Eminent Victorians*; and Leonard Woolf (1880-1969), publisher of the Hogarth Press and husband of Virginia Woolf (1882-1941). The poet Rupert Brooke (1887-1915) was one of the few members to support the war; he died from an infection following a mosquito bite and was buried on a Greek island.

The Society is of interest for two other reasons. First, up until the Great War, the circle was influential in politics as well as literature and philosophy; some 14 per cent were members of Parliament. Secondly, it was closely associated with the Bloomsbury group, the name given to a group of friends living in or near the London district of Bloomsbury from 1905 to 1939. There was a large overlapping membership between the Bloomsbury Group and the Apostles; of the thirteen Bloomsbury members, nine of the ten men were Cambridge alumni, mostly Apostles. They were united by their friendship and by their common interest in arts, literature, and politics. Professor W. C. Lubenow has described their interconnections as:

> Like the Apostles, Bloomsbury had no common ideas about art, literature, or politics. Like the Apostles, nothing mattered to Bloomsbury so long as one was honest. Like the Apostles, Bloomsbury was engaged in a moral adventure. Like the Apostles, Bloomsbury saw through the humbug of family. Like the Apostles, Bloomsbury was marked by candid discussion in which high seriousness, gossip, gaiety, and argument were all mixed together.[4]

Intellectual Development

The Bloomsbury Group's first location was at 46 Gordon Square, where one of their neighbours was Dr Williams Library, established by nonconformist dissenters and housed in the former London University Hall since 1890. This location would become more significant to Norman Murray Bell when he pursued his divinity studies at London University.

The academic community of Trinity College was residential and well integrated. Norman Murray Bell would have been aware he was rubbing shoulders with members of the Apostles who were intellectual leaders in avant-garde ideas and social criticism; and that they also comprised most of the Bloomsbury group. In a few short years, great power rivalries would begin to dominate international relations. At their core, the Apostles and members of the Bloomsbury group were internationalists and pacifists, "convinced that most wars were neither just nor necessary, and that the First World War was one of them."[5] They were opposed to conscription when it was introduced in Britain. However, the conviction and later jailing of Bertrand Russell for his pacifist activities, resulting in the subsequent loss of his Trinity College lectureship[6] was a source of conflict within the Apostles. Norman Murray Bell could not have known as he left Cambridge University that he was to be drawn into this vortex in a few short years.

University of London, 1912-1915

Norman Murray Bell had a three-year scholarship from New Zealand and had finished his Cambridge degree in two years. He was determined to see and do as much as he could while the opportunity was there, in his remarkable pursuit of knowledge. London University offered an ideal prospect: he could enrol as an external student while continuing to work and study at other locations. It also allowed him to study divinity, a subject that had interested him since his days at Christ's College, at a large university with an excellent reputation. This was important, as the smaller denominational theological colleges, usually not affiliated to a university, were often unknown outside their denomination, sometimes wracked with painful theological disputes and of variable scholastic standard. Biblical criticism, modernism, and Darwinism all took their toll on teachers at any number of dissenting theological colleges. Two of the leading nonconformist theological colleges had already moved to Oxford in the late nineteenth century, Mansfield College in 1886 and Manchester College in 1889. Both moves had been facilitated by the passing of the Universities Tests Act 1871 which abolished religious tests at Oxford, Cambridge, and Durham universities.

The University of London's Faculty of Theology was created in 1900 when two important dissenting theological academies, New College and Hackney College, became constituent parts of the Faculty. Professor Alfred Cave, who had been principal of Hackney College since 1881, took a leading part in creating the new Faculty.[7] Professor Cave was quite orthodox in his outlook and "continued to hold and defend traditional views".[8] New College, on the other hand, had attracted many leading thinkers from the Congregationalist, Calvinist, and Reformed church traditions.

When Norman Murray Bell enrolled in the Faculty of Theology in 1912, the Faculty's academic staff were drawn from various theology departments and other colleges, in addition to New College and Hackney College; including Kings College, Wesleyan College at Richmond, Regents Park College, and St John's Hall.[9] From July 1912, when he became a student, until he completed his BD in 1914, Norman Murray Bell studied the same subjects and took the same examinations as internal students. His intermediate examinations were in elementary Hebrew and New Testament Greek, Classical Greek, Latin, Psychology and Philosophy. The degree subjects were Old Testament, New Testament, Biblical and Historical Theology, Church History, Philosophical Introduction to Theology, and a choice of one subject from Church History, Patristic or Scholastic Texts, the Comparative Study of Religions, and Christian Ethics.[10] Bell elected to re-enrol in 1915 for honours and chose to sit an examination in the subject the Study of Religion, receiving a first-class pass.[11] (To obtain an honours degree required a first-class pass in at least three papers and Bell did not complete this requirement.) The study of religion, especially comparative religion, was now playing an increasingly critical part in his thinking. He was also drawn into consideration of the unfolding devastation unleashed by the Great War. These were serious issues that he would develop during the remainder of his time overseas and that would be a cause of further action upon his return to New Zealand.

The Theistic Church and the Free Religious Movement

Studying religion allowed Norman Murray Bell to explore many interests, especially in the areas of comparative religion, Christian ethics and radical ideas which were sometimes considered expressions of heretical thought. The Theistic Church and the Free Religious Movement both fitted well with Norman Murray Bell's studies; students of religion in Bell's day had heard of Charles Voysey, the founder of the Theistic Church, and his successor Walter Walsh. In an address to his church in Dundee in 1912 Dr Walsh declared the "beginning of a Movement towards Free Religion" which would have no creed, ordinances or sacraments.[12] Given Norman Murray Bell's attraction to comparative religion and the theological basis of his pacifism, which would consume his later life, he would have been intensely interested in both of these religious movements.

In 1869 the trial of the Rev. Charles Voysey (1828-1912) an Anglican Vicar in Yorkshire and broad churchman, was a *cause célèbre*. Voysey was a graduate of St Edmund Hall, Oxford, and had been ordained a priest in the Church of England in 1853. In 1863 he published a series of sermons denying eternal punishment. While the church establishment may have been inclined to overlook this obvious heresy, a lay group, the Church Association, would not, and raised money to finance a prosecution. The trial was held in York Minster in 1869 and Voysey was convicted. He then appealed to the Privy Council, with the defence costs being met by subscription of his backers, including another broad churchman, Benjamin Jowett, Master of Balliol College at Oxford. In 1871 the appeal was denied and Voysey was deprived of his living or clerical orders.[13]

Later in 1871, Charles Voysey held a public meeting attended by 163 people, including Charles Darwin (1809-1882) and John William Colenso (1814-1883), the liberal Bishop of Natal, who had faced the charge of heresy and won his case on appeal. This meeting established the Theistic Church with Voysey its minister. Two thousand attended the first service on 1 October 1871 and many were turned away. Later the church found a permanent home in the old Huguenot Chapel in Swallow Street, just off Regent Street in central London, where it

Chapter 2

Charles Voysey *Walter Walsh*

remained until 1912.[14] Voysey attracted support from many notable people, including the Norwegian composer Edvard Grieg during the six months he was living in England. Grieg had found new friends who had a profound effect on his religious outlook.[15]

When Charles Voysey died in 1912 he was succeeded at Swallow Street by the Rev. Dr Walter Walsh (1857-1931), who was educated at Glasgow University and the University of Pittsburgh, where he received his DD in 1910. He was minister at the Gilfillan Memorial Church, Dundee (a Congregational church) from 1897 to 1912. At an early stage he made public his pacifist views in *The Moral Damage of War*, which he published in 1902 in response to the South African war.[16] He occupied this very liberal pulpit in his home town until he was condemned for Universalist views by the Court of Sessions in Edinburgh in 1912 and deprived of church properties. Following the case in 1912, he formed the Free Religious Movement in Dundee. Like the similarly named Free Religious Association, which was formed in America in 1867 as a "spiritual anti-slavery society" to emancipate religion from its dogmatic traditions and oppose doctrinal tendencies within Unitarianism,[17] the Free Religious Movement in the twentieth century was driven by anti-war advocacy in which it thought traditional churches were not adequately engaged. Both organisations then developed similar broader positions beyond their respective initial driving forces.

Early in 1913, only a few months after founding the Free Religious Movement, Dr Walsh accepted an invitation to succeed the late Rev. Voysey as minister at the Theistic Church. Three years later, on 31 October 1916, his ministry was terminated because his pacifism clashed with the Theistic Church's support for the war. Supported by his friends and members of his former congregation, Dr Walsh formed the Free Religious Movement in London. After a few moves to different locations, the Free Religious Movement finally settled into Lindsey Hall at Notting Hill Gate, where it remained throughout Walter Walsh's ministry.

The Free Religious Movement was religious in a broad ethical sense: it encouraged acceptance of universalism in religion and social ethics and politics, where it sided with the rights and needs of the poor and workers. Dr Walsh attracted a following into the Free Religious Movement largely composed of Free Christians, Ethicists, Unitarians, Quakers, Socialists, educational reformers, animal welfare advocates, vegetarians, and pacifists. His was a church without creed, sacrament, or ordinances, but its theology was a belief in pure theism. It asserted that everyone had the right to speak their thoughts and so ensured intellectual freedom. One of the movement's strongest beliefs was the advocacy of pacifism. Dr Walsh wrote and spoke on this topic many times. He was vice-president of the Universal Peace Union. This was a pacifist organisation formed in Rhode Island in 1866, which had amongst its American founders a notable minister and reformer, Adin Ballou (1803-1890), an advocate of peace and Christian non-violence.[18]

Norman Murray Bell could have visited the Theistic Church in London in 1912, when Voysey was still in charge, or later when it was led by Walter Walsh. He could have visited the Free Religious Movement either in Dundee or London. When Bell arrived at St Andrews in 1914 the Free Religious Movement was still functioning at Dundee. The following year Walsh took over the Theistic Church and three years later in 1916 formed a Free Religious Movement in London. It is most likely that Norman Murray Bell was already familiar with the Free Religious Movement by the time he returned to New Zealand in 1916. Bell wrote his theological basis for peace, *A Gospel of Universal Compassion Being Another Side of*

Chapter 2

Christianity,[19] the ideas of which are congruent with the religious pacifism espoused by Walter Walsh, before his return to New Zealand.

It is possible that Bell became familiar with the Free Religious Movement during the first few years following his return to New Zealand, but this is less likely. A digital search of New Zealand newspapers between the beginning of 1916 and the end of 1925 found only two mentions of Walter Walsh and one of the Free Religious Movement.[20] If, however, he had not become acquainted with the Free Religious Movement or the Theistic Church before leaving England, he could have heard about them from two New Zealand clergymen who were overseas at the time of his return, the Rev. James Chapple (1865-1947) and Rev. Frederick Sinclaire (1881-1954). These two men were destined to play a significant role in his future.

University of Liverpool, 1913-1914

Following his success at Trinity College, Bell wanted to undertake further work in chemistry. His Tutor at Cambridge, William Cecil Dampier Whetham, was in a unique position to help him. He was married to Catherine Durning Holt (1871-1952), daughter of Robert Durning Holt, whose family owned the Blue Funnel Shipping Line. The Holts were members of the Unitarian church and generous benefactors to educational, health and welfare bodies in Liverpool. Catherine's nephew was Dr Alfred Holt (1877-1931), Reader in Physical Chemistry

Alfred Holt

Intellectual Development

Muspratt Laboratory, Liverpool University

at the Muspratt Laboratory of Physical and Electrochemistry, part of the University of Liverpool. From its foundation, Liverpool University had established positions in chemistry and became known as a centre that attracted highly qualified staff in this area.[21] It was an excellent choice for Norman Murray Bell.

Alfred Holt had studied at Pembroke College, University of Cambridge, from 1897, taking the Natural Science Tripos. He received his BA in 1900 and MA in 1905. From 1909 to 1912 he was an assistant lecturer in chemistry at the University of Manchester. He graduated from Manchester with an MSc in chemistry in 1907 and a DSc in 1909. Beginning in 1902 Holt had carried out a great deal of research, first working with Professor Henri Moissan in Paris, where they jointly authored papers on silicides of vanadium, then continuing at Manchester, where he read papers before the Royal Society and the Literary and Philosophical Society on various aspects of chemistry. He published papers in the *Journal of The Chemical Society*. His best-known research was into the absorption of hydrogen by palladium. Dr Holt's appointment to a Readership at the University of Liverpool in 1912 was further recognition of his distinguished record of original research.

Norman Murray Bell was a Graduate Research Student in residence for the academic years 1913-1914 in the Faculty of Science at the University of Liverpool.[22] He was likely provided with residence at the men's hostel in Croxteth Road, known as the Ashton Rathbone Hostel. Admission to pursue original research at the University Laboratories depended on the recommendation of the Head of Department concerned, in this case, Dr Holt. Shortly after his arrival Bell had a paper published in a prestigious German chemistry journal, entitled in English translation: "The Velocity of Evolution of Oxygen from Bleaching Powder Solutions in the Presence of Small Quantities of Cobalt Nitrate and the Influence of Different Compounds on it."[23] (This appears to be the first time his proficiency in the German language resulted in a publication.) At the beginning of 1914, Dr Holt and Norman Murray Bell published their research in the *Journal of the Chemical Society Transactions*.[24]

Britain declared war on Germany on 4 August 1914 and the chemical department of the university became the headquarters in the northwestern area for the chemical testing of explosives. Dr Holt was appointed chief assistant to the deputy inspector of high explosives and in that role was the technical examiner of explosive factories in the area. This was to be the first involvement of Norman Murray Bell with war work at a university where he was undertaking chemistry research.

University of St Andrews, 1914-1915

For the academic year 1914-1915 Norman Murray Bell was a research student at the University of St Andrews in Fife, Scotland. Founded early in the fifteenth century by a small group of Augustinian clergy who were expelled from Paris for religious schism and excluded from England by the Anglo-Scottish wars, St Andrews was the third oldest university in the English-speaking world, after Cambridge and Oxford. Important developments at St Andrews in the late nineteenth century were the eligibility for women to receive an education equal to men in 1889, and the merger with University College, Dundee in 1897, with its attention on scientific and professional courses.

Intellectual Development

United College courtyard, St Andrews University

St Andrews held a particular attraction for Norman Murray Bell. Studying there meant returning to his family's Scottish roots: both his mother and his paternal grandfather had emigrated to New Zealand from Scotland. Norman Murray Bell inherited the traditions of Clan Bell from his father, and his Glasgow-born mother kept the Scottish heritage alive amongst her sons. (The motto of Clan Bell, *Signum Pacis Amor* or Love is the token of Peace, is particularly appropriate for a man who would dedicate his life to the pursuit of peace.)

St Andrews was also the institution where the Scottish-American philanthropist and peace advocate Andrew Carnegie (1835-1919) had been Lord Rector from 1901 to 1907. In 1905 he gave an address to the students entitled *A League of Peace*,[25] which attracted widespread attention for its call for peace and the abolition of war, tracing these sentiments from ancient to modern times. The speech included a report on The Hague Conference and the proposal to establish a World Court to settle international disputes. It was a far-sighted report that proposed the formation of a League of Peace

Chapter 2

Andrew Carnegie

which all nations could join, agreeing that no nation would go to war. It was an idea ahead of its time but one that, as we will see, came to pass in the 1920s. Carnegie's ideas foreshadowed the League of Nations that would be formed after the war. He established the Carnegie Endowment for International Peace in 1910, a $10 million fund to be used to abolish war. He was a major donor to the International Court of Arbitration's Peace Palace in The Hague, and in 1914, on the eve of the Great War, he founded the Church Peace Union, bringing together leaders of religion, academia, and politics. Andrew Carnegie had been affected by the religious strife he had witnessed in Scotland and rejected organised religion. Later in life, his firm opposition to orthodoxy moderated and he attended a local Presbyterian church in America that expounded the Social Gospel. His views and advocacy would have been well known to Norman Murray Bell.

By the time Norman Murray Bell had completed his enrolment the Great War had been underway for three months. He was granted residence at United College. First, he asked for admission to carry out research work in education, a new subject for him. His proposed research topic was "Early contributions to the theory and practice of Education with special reference to Plato's Laws and Dialogues other than the Republic." Professor Edgar of the Faculty of Arts offered to supervise his research for two years. The second part of this application was to recognise his existing degrees as satis-

Intellectual Development

Professor James Irvine

fying the requirements to become a candidate for the DPhil degree after the proposed two years of research, which was granted.[26] He was successful in his educational research, winning the Education Medal. He did not proceed with a doctorate, possibly because of the uncertainty caused by the war, although he may already have intended to study on the continent. He did, however, use his educational research later in New Zealand when he published *Education For Freedom* and proclaimed on the cover "Late Research Student in Education, University of St. Andrews, Scotland."[27]

During his time at St Andrews Norman Murray Bell worked in the chemistry laboratory. Presumably, he had been assisted with an introduction by Dr Alfred Holt. (Though this has not been formally documented, there are several photographs of the St Andrews Chemistry Laboratory and staff in the photo album held in the Norman Murray Bell collection at Christchurch Public Library and two contemporary New Zealand newspaper reports state he "is now studying education and chemistry at St. Andrew's University, Scotland."[28])

Academically St Andrews offered Norman Murray Bell the chance to work with a well-known chemist who was undertaking work of a highly innovative nature in the field of what would become military medicine, something that he found more palatable than munitions. The Chemistry Department was led by renowned organic chemist Professor James

Chapter 2

Colquhoun Irvine (1877-1952). James Irvine had graduated from St Andrews with a BSc then studied for his PhD at the University of Leipzig. He then returned to St Andrews and was awarded a DSc degree. He became Professor of Chemistry in 1909 and Dean of Science in 1912. Later he was appointed Principal of St Andrews University and University College, Dundee. His discoveries in carbohydrate chemistry helped unlock "ring structures" of the carbohydrates. This work contributed to developments in biology such as the discovery of DNA. During the war Professor Irvine led a team that developed drugs that protected troops from meningitis; produced the local anaesthetic novocaine, and developed drugs to mitigate the effects of mustard gas.

Unlike Norman Murray Bell's sojourn at Liverpool University which resulted in three scientific publications, he did not write about his chemistry research at St Andrews, either while there or later in New Zealand. However, on 11 May 1915, Bell read a paper at the meeting of the Faraday Society in the rooms of the Chemical Society at Burlington House, London, with the President, Sir Robert Hadfield, in the chair.[29] Bell's paper "On the Anodic Solution of Lead", the culmination of his chemistry research at the Muspratt Laboratory at Liverpool, was later published in the *Faraday Transactions*[30]; a singular recognition of the abilities of this young New Zealander.

War Workers, Chemical Laboratory, St Andrews University, summer 1915

Intellectual Development

When word of Norman Murray Bell's chemistry work at Liverpool and St Andrews universities reached home, there was an unforeseen effect. Because of the patriotic fervour the war engendered it was assumed that Bell would be working for the war effort. Newspaper reports claimed that he was "employed in chemical research work for the British Government in connexion with the war."[31] The same report gave an account of his brother Harold (1890-1958) "who was among the first to land at the Dardanelles, and who was wounded on May 8, is now convalescent, but expresses himself eager to rejoin his company at the front." This was not the end of the expectations newspapers reported about Norman Murray Bell. It was claimed that "Mr. Norman M. Bell is in training in the Old Country, and expects to receive a commission in Kitchener's Army."[32]

University of Bern and Return to New Zealand, 1915-1916

Since the outbreak of war in 1914 it would have been virtually impossible for Norman Murray Bell to enter Germany to study at Heidelberg University. He was travelling on a British passport and would have been considered an enemy alien.[33] In 1915, however, Bell managed to travel and enroll at the University of Bern without any problem, probably going by train across France. Switzerland was a neutral country during the Great War, although surrounded by the Central Powers of Germany and Austria-Hungary to the east and the Allied countries of France and Italy on the western and southern borders respectively. Bern

University of Bern, main building

Chapter 2

was regarded as the de facto capital in the Swiss Federal political system and had attracted many pacifists during the war. Between 26 October 1915 and 27 July 1916 Norman Murray Bell was a regular student in the Faculty of Science.[34] His fluency in German would have been helpful at university, as this was the majority spoken language. The university archive does not provide information on his studies; however, chemistry was one of the subjects he could have studied.

Shortly after his return to London, Norman Murray Bell found a berth on the *SS Ionic*, arriving in Auckland on 3 October 1916, continuing on its voyage to Lyttelton, where Bell disembarked a few days later. He had been away for seven years, and during that time had matured as an academic and scientist, experienced published researcher, theologically proficient and an ethicist. He was twenty-nine years old.

3

War and Resistance

Theology, Conscientious Objection,
Imprisonment and Return to Society, 1916-1919

Arriving Home

We can safely assume that Norman Murray Bell's parents, Annie and Horace, were on the dockside waiting to meet Norman on his arrival at Lyttelton Port in 1916, looking forward to seeing their son after so many years away. The family would then have travelled to Christchurch by train and made their way home to Cumberland Street, Richmond, a central city suburb.

It must have been a homecoming with unexpected discoveries made after familial relationships had been resumed. One of Norman's brothers, Harold, was serving overseas with the New Zealand Army. When he joined up on the outbreak of war in 1914 he gave Anglican as his religion. Having been wounded in action in the Gallipoli campaign in 1915, he was wounded again in France in September 1916 and transferred to England for hospital treatment. A year later their youngest brother Wilfred would enlist, giving his religion as Methodist, and like his older brother be wounded in action.

Very soon after his return the family would learn their eldest son, far from receiving a commission in the Army as they may have imagined, had no intention of joining the fight. In fact, the only fight he wanted to join was opposition to the war. The jingoistic spirit was strong in the Empire countries and could cause fear within the family of any defaulter

Chapter 3

Norman Murray Bell (seated) and his brother Harold

who refused to serve. The famous New Zealand novelist Frank Sargeson (1903-1982) wrote about how this fear threatened his family:

> Once, towards the end of the last war, we were badly frightened. There was a chance of our father's having to go. He was near the age limit, but he had to fill in a paper saying whether he'd be willing to go or not. We never said anything to each other but we were frightened. We were frightened too that our father would say on the paper that he wasn't willing to go. That was our worse fear.[1]

Did the resulting family discord result in Norman Murray Bell leaving home for a while to give his parents time to adjust to their son's views? This is a possibility, especially considering one of Norman's first acts on returning to New Zealand was to arrange publication of *A Gospel of Universal Compassion*. Although Norman Murray Bell would write in a letter in 1928 that "The pamphlet was published about the beginning of 1916",[2] as he was still in Europe at that time it could not have been published till the end of that year or early in the next.

A Gospel of Universal Compassion and Nonconformist Theology

A Gospel of Universal Compassion is the theological basis for Norman Murray Bell's rejection of war and all forms of violence.

The following is a summary of this 20-page monograph. The language has been adjusted to make it more gender-neutral. It contains numerous Biblical references, not all of which are cited in the summary. (Bell noted in the introduction that he translated New Testament passages from Westcott and Hort's edition of the original Greek, with constant cross-reference to the Moffatt translation.)

Bell's analysis began from the premiss that the goal of the religious person is the attainment of eternal life, which, according to Jesus, is a life of particular quality. Therefore the most important event in a person's life occurs at the day of judgement, because that is when the question of eternal life is decided. Whether a person enters into eternal life or eternal punishment depends simply on whether he or she has done or neglected to do certain acts (Matt. 25: 42-43). It is, in Bell's view, a question of deeds, not of beliefs. On the day of judgement the deeds that matter are acts of compassion done to even the least of the King's brothers — the King being

Chapter 3

the Son of Man, Jesus (Matt. 25: 37-46, Luke 14: 12-24). Who then are the King's brothers? (Matt. 25: 34-40) In the final analysis all people are God's sons and daughters; they are all included when the King points to the least of these as being his brethren (Acts 10: 33, Luke 6: 35). Based on this analysis, Bell concluded that what matters on the day of judgement are acts of universal compassion (Matt. 12: 33-34). It is, he said, in "exhibiting such an unlimited compassion that one acts like God." In support of this he cited "God is kind to unjust and wicked men" (Luke 6: 35) and "You must be perfect as your heavenly Father is perfect" (Matt. 5: 48).

Bell next referred to the Biblical injunctions to love your enemies and do good to those that hate you, hoping for nothing from the act, and to love your neighbour as yourself (Luke 6: 27-36 and Mark 12: 31). This love, which Norman Murray Bell understood as compassion, leaves no room for anger (Matt. 5: 23-24, James 1: 26); only unlimited forgiveness is permissible. Not only should evildoers not be resisted with force, but all wrongs should be endured without complaint (1 Thess. 5: 15, 1 Peter 2: 19-24). To carry compassion to this extent it is necessary to love even one's enemies (Mark 12: 31). "By so acting, man attains the perfection of God, and shows himself for what he is, sons of the Most High" ("a rich reward", Luke 6: 36). Next, Bell argued that there is a Biblical concept of a Kingdom of God embracing all people and all nationalities, united by a common bond of compassion or love, which is shown to all in need. And Jesus is the King of this realm, though in the world his position was to wear a scarlet robe and a crown of thorns (Mark 15: 17). The members of this Kingdom put their principle of universal compassion first, and sooner than surrender that they would give up their family and even their lives (Luke 14: 26-27). According to Johannine teaching, a person who loves his brother remains in the light but one who hates his or her brother is in darkness (1 John 2: 9-11). God is love (or compassion) (1 John 4: 7) and this love is the life of people. In loving one knows God, so that one who loves has "absolute confidence concerning the day of judgement" (1 John 4: 17). Bell's conclusion was that humanity is related to God by birth and character as children of God; any person can be the son or daughter of God if by habitual disposition they are full of love toward humanity showing unlimited compassion. Such a person has already attained the goal of the religious person — that is, eternal life.

War and Resistance

Norman Murray Bell even stated his basic thesis in a form that might appeal to those who did not share the Christian perspective. "In non-religious terms: The life most worth living is that of the man who so loves his fellowman that the latter's need always calls forth from him unlimited deeds of compassion." Such a world view is consistent with Albert Schweitzer's "absolute ethic of reverence for life."[3] In September 1915, while on a two hundred kilometre journey up the Ogowe River in N'Gomo, the words "Reverence for Life" suddenly came to Schweitzer as the elementary and universal conception of ethics for which he had been seeking. Upon this principle his whole philosophy of civilization was subsequently based.[4] It was serendipitous that these two ethicists, Albert Schweitzer and Norman Murray Bell, were thinking along similar lines at approximately the same time. There is an appendix following the conclusion, which mainly deals with the origin and reliability of New Testament texts, the implications for Norman Murray Bell's contentions, and some other considerations of Biblical interpretation.

How congruous is *A Gospel of Universal Compassion* with the theology of nonconformity? What can we learn from these principles about the

Albert Schweitzer

varieties of nonconformity that may be consistent or inconsistent with Norman Murray Bell's approach to theology?

We begin with the position of individual conscience, as this appears to be the bedrock of nonconformist thinking. The Reformation started when the Augustinian friar Martin Luther (1483-1546) published his *Ninety-Five Theses* in 1517, an act which was to fundamentally undermine the very idea of church authority. Luther disputed the Papal right to issue indulgences and was excommunicated by Pope Leo X. The resulting enforcement of the ban on the *Ninety-Five Theses* was a secular affair held at the Diet of Worms. There Martin Luther gave his famous response to his protagonists, putting conscience above authority:

> Unless I am convinced by the testimony of the Scriptures or by clear reason (for I do not trust either in the pope or in councils alone since it is well known that they have often erred and contradicted themselves), I am bound by the Scriptures I have quoted and my conscience is captive to the Word of God. I cannot and will not recant anything, since it is neither safe nor right to go against conscience. May God help me. Amen.[5]

The Diet condemned Luther for his errors and declared him a heretic, which made it a crime to assist him, but not a crime to kill him. However, Luther found a secret protector in Prince Frederick, the Elector of Saxony, who arranged his safe passage to and from Worms and had him taken to safety in Wartburg Castle at Eisenach. Luther was to refer to this period of exile as his Patmos, referring to the Greek Island where John is said to have written the Book of Revelation (see Revelation 1: 9), arguably the most political book in the Bible.

The Reformation which began with Luther sparked a process of change which — whatever the intention of its instigator — ended up fatally destabilising the authority of the Church. Luther's challenge came at a time when there was also a challenge from secular political forces, which would eventually lead to the fracturing of Christendom. Luther made a compelling argument for the primacy of individual conscience, which would in time come to include the rejection of absolute authority over the individual's political conscience as well as religious conscience. Eventually these ideas would emerge as fundamental concepts in the legal system of the modern western secular state.[6] Those who appeal to the right of individual conscience can also point to the teaching of Thomas Aquinas (1225-1274), who said that everyone has to believe and act in accord with one's conscience, or as Paul put it: "Let everyone be fully convinced in his own mind" (Romans 14:5) and "Why should my liberty be determined by someone else's conscience?" (1 Corinthians 10:29).

The two principles of Luther's theology that combine over time were the transcending concept of *sola scriptura*, by scripture alone, and *sola fide*, by faith alone in contrast to good works. *Sola scriptura* rejects any authority other than the Bible and makes the Bible the test by which claims of authority are to be measured. *Sola scriptura* is a formal principle of many Protestant Christian churches, particularly evangelical denominations. Anglican and Methodist churches hold to the position of *prima scriptura*, which allows for tradition, reason and experience to help in understanding scripture. *Sola fide* is part of the historical context of Luther's avowal of justification by faith. "Salvation therefore, if it is by grace alone, becomes ours *through faith alone*."[7] Justification by faith has become the doctrine most closely associated with Luther's legacy. However, Luther's challenge to the moral authority of the Catholic Church had unintended and unforeseen consequences. Once individuals were able to act in accordance with the dictates of their conscience, it brought into question the right of any authority to exercise power over people. These tendencies went far beyond what Luther had intended with his reforms of corrupt practices within the Papacy, but once the genie was out of the bottle there was no turning back.

The Reformed churches of the sixteenth century were derived from two traditions. The first was Lutheran, often adopted as state or national churches in some German states, Denmark, Norway, Sweden, Finland, Latvia, Estonia and Iceland. The other is the Calvinist tradition, arising from the reforms of John Calvin, Huldrych Zwingli and John Knox; this was established in some other German states, Holland, Switzerland, France and Scotland. With the rejection of papal jurisdiction in England by King Henry VIII in 1534 and the Scottish reformation in 1560 the Protestant Reformation spread to Britain, and state churches were established there. Churches in the Reformed tradition maintained as part of their theology the notion of just war, a doctrine derived from the Catholic Church.

Before the Roman Emperor Constantine (272-337) converted to Christianity in the fourth century, Christians in the Roman Empire did not become soldiers. This was due to two factors: the tendency of the early church Fathers to condemn all war as sinful; and the rejection by the Christian church of the cult of the emperor as a god. However, the development of the just war theory by St Augustine (354-430), Bishop of Hippo, shed a new light on the question of whether a Christian could bear arms for the emperor. Augustine declared as a first principle that the final object of war is peace. He defined wars as just when they aim to avenge injury: that is, when the people or city against whom war is to be declared had neglected either to redress serious and lasting injuries done by its subjects, or to restore what they have wrongfully seized. All other means to obtain redress must have been ineffective; success must be very likely and the force used must not produce evils greater than the evils to be eliminated. Augustine condemned unjust war as robbery on a majestic scale. There was also a principle of justice during war, to ensure that once war began it should not be conducted unjustly, such as by indiscriminate killing and destruction.[8]

The theory of Augustine was expanded and refined by Thomas Aquinas, who declared in his *Summa Theologica* that for war to be just it must be instituted by a proper authority, such as the state; there must be a good and just purpose in going to war; and finally, peace must be the central motive for the war, even in the midst of violence. However, it is possible that Aquinas also incorporated a pacifist position into his just war doctrine, based on his interpretation of Matthew 5:39 ("Do not resist evil ...."). A plausible contention has been put forward that Aquinas had a two-stage theory. The first stage was the rejection of pacifism by the state, while the second affirmed pacifism as a suitable response to evil by the church. "This split vision, whereby the justifiability of armed violence was both affirmed and denied, was derivative upon the distinction ... between the things of God and the things of Caesar."[9]

Following the main Reformation a smaller radical reformation took place, initially in Germany and Switzerland. These reformers, most of whom were Anabaptists, believed that the first Reformation had not gone far enough; that the church should not be involved with the state in any way. For the Anabaptists belief was a matter of individual conscience and could not be forced on anyone. Typically Anabaptism has been associated with pacifism, especially in its Mennonite branch.

Another significant development that would later impact the question of just war versus pacifism grew out of controversy within the Church of England. In 1662 there occurred the "Great Ejection" from the Anglican Church of the Puritans, those for whom individual conscience was more important than the national church. The Act of Uniformity required all clergy to swear an oath to use only rites and ceremonies contained in the *Book of Common Prayer*, to accept episcopal ordination of all ministers by the Church of England and never to seek change in the church or state. Consequently, about 2,000 clergymen were ejected from the established church for failing to comply with the Act. Thereafter English Presbyterians, Congregationalists, and Baptists were identified as non-conformist; and as other denominations formed, including Methodist, Unitarian, Quaker, Plymouth Brethren (or Christian Brethren, as they preferred to be called) and English Moravian, they became part of the non-conformist tradition. Many Presbyterian congregations underwent growing heterodoxy, becoming Christian Unitarian.

Within the British nonconformist tradition, the known peace churches included Anabaptist, Mennonite, Brethren[10] and Quaker. (Moravian non-combatancy did not extend to complete pacifism and allowed for self-defence). However the organisational laxity amongst other denominations allowed individual members and individual churches to embrace a peace position as they wished. This provided the impetus for the Society for the Promotion of Permanent and Universal Peace, formed in London in June 1816. Membership was nondenominational. Quaker influence was strong, though membership included Methodists, Congregationalists, Baptists, Unitarians, and Anglicans, both clergy and lay. Only the Catholics were aloof. The Peace Society initiated a series of international conferences advocating arbitration to resolve disputes. The first was held in London in 1843. Three more Universal Peace Congresses were held: in Brussels in 1848, Paris in 1849 and London in 1851. The American Peace Society, which had been founded in 1815, was weakened by the Civil War; as the Crimean War affected the Peace Society in England. Although the London Peace Society continued, by 1914 it was no longer the dominant voice it had once been.[11]

From this we can see how Norman Murray Bell's theological pacifist reasoning fits into the larger pacifist tradition. The major Catholic and

Chapter 3

Protestant church positions, which adopted just war theory, are incompatible with his views. His theological position closely aligns with the second radical reformation, from which the Anabaptist-Mennonites emerged, together with the Puritan peace churches that were part of the nonconformist tradition following the Great Ejection. Such an orientation is compatible with the scholarly direction he would likely have experienced at the Faculty of Theology, London University, especially amongst the teachers from New College. What may have been uncommon in his theological position was the linking of pacifist texts and arguments with the attainment of eternal life by doing God's will. However, the supremacy of conscience and the authority of Biblical texts are the basis of his position.

It is noteworthy that the writings of Norman Murray Bell say nothing about the history of the war traditions found in the Old Testament. The many descriptions of extreme violence, often carried out against innocent men, women and children and domestic animals, were sanctioned and at times instigated by the Hebrew God. At times whole cities were ordered reduced to rubble. There is little significant evaluation of war ethics to be found in the Old Testament. War is often described simply in terms of divine judgement.[12] Norman Murray Bell did not resile from this complete contradiction to his theological position. He ignored it. Perhaps he would have said that the commandments contained in the New Testament swept away those in the Old.

By the time Norman Murray Bell enrolled for his honours paper "The Study of Religion" in 1915, the Great War was well underway. For many, the nonconformist conscience had started to fray during the South African wars, when it lost its single-minded commitment to peace. By 1914 the dreadfulness of what was in train was apparent to those who saw beyond the naïve jingoistic appeal to King and Empire and considered the ethical and humanitarian implications of war. It is no wonder that such an intelligent young man as Norman Murray Bell produced this advanced theological treatise in 1916. It tells us how politically aware he had become and how deeply he had thought about the greatest ethical issue facing his generation, that of human violence on an unprecedented scale. He was not dissuaded by popular pressure from advocating an unpopular proposal. Shortly his beliefs would be put to the test.

Teaching and Defying the Army

It is likely that between arriving at Lyttelton in October 1916 and his appointment to a teaching position at Christchurch Boys' High School in March 1917, Norman Murray Bell spent his time putting final touches to his monograph *A Gospel of Universal Compassion* and arranging for its publication. He was staying at his parents' house at 31 Cumberland Street, Richmond, a well-off middle-class suburb. He found a full-time position from 1 March 1917 as temporary assistant master and science demonstrator at Christchurch Boys' High School. The school seemed happy to have recruited such a well-qualified teacher, as they reported his appointment "Mr N. M. Bell, who has been till recently at the University of Berne..."[13] even though he lacked any high school teaching experience. Within three months of starting his new job, Norman Murray Bell began advertising as a private tutor in the local newspapers. He specified his academic qualifications, namely honours in classics at Cambridge and theology at London. Additionally he stated he was a research student in chemistry at Liverpool and education at St Andrews and finally a candidate in philosophy at Bern. The special subjects he offered to tutor in for matriculation or university examinations were Latin, Greek, Chemistry, German, French and Education.[14] Subsequent advertisements were simpler, listing his degrees and offering tutoring services. Within a fortnight he added an address in the advertisements, at Hereford Street, a main street in the city, across the Avon River from his parents' house. He was using this address as an office, which must have increased the costs of his business, unless it was provided by a friend rent-free. He may have needed to earn more income to repay debts, possibly from family loans, as his finances during the long period in Europe would have been uncertain at best: some scholarship money and possibly small stipends when a research assistant. He also needed money to live on during the first six months after he returned home.

During July 1917 Norman Murray Bell wrote a letter to the *Maoriland Worker* (a publication for working-class people on the left of the political spectrum) entering a debate about how different classes of conscientious objectors were treated: those with religious convictions were eligible for

Chapter 3

an exemption, while those without were made to bear the full penalty of the law.[15] Even on a religious basis there was a very limited ground for exemption. The Military Service Act provided for those who could prove before the outbreak of war they had been members of a church that had in its written constitution the requirement not to bear arms. Effectively, this limited exemptions to the Society of Friends and the Christadelphians. But Norman Murray Bell thought "we all should be treated alike".[16] Presumably this meant those with a religious objection far broader than provided for, as well as those with an ethical objection not religiously based and those who thought the inequities of war fell too heavily on the working classes.

The test for Norman Murray Bell came soon enough. On 28 August 1917, Bell was one of three religious objectors who were arrested for failing to comply with the requirements of the Military Service Act. He was then transferred to Trentham Military Camp, where on 30 August 1917 he received twenty-eight days' detention for refusing to be medically examined. It is noteworthy that Bell had not applied for exemption from service under the Act, as he might have done, given his strong religious conscientious objection to being involved in war. Upon completion of the period of detention, he refused to follow the command of an officer to pick up his kit, and on 13 October 1917 he was convicted, by court-martial held at Trentham Military Camp, of the charge of disobeying a lawful command given by his superior officer. For this offence he was given a sentence of two years' imprisonment with hard labour,[17] which he served at Rotoaira Prison, south of Lake Taupo. There prisoners were put to work on constructing roads.

Bell was released on 13 April 1919. As he had not appeared before the Religious Objectors Advisory Board as part of his stand against the unfairness of the treatment of conscientious objectors, he was placed on the military defaulters list. His was one of 2,373 names on a list, published in 1919, of military defaulters who were deprived of their civil rights for ten years. (Ninety-nine names were subsequently removed on appeal and forty-six names were added, making the final total 2,320. Of these, 286 objectors were imprisoned between early 1917 and 11 November 1918: of these, 49 per cent held religious objections to war, 21 per cent held socialist objections and 4 per cent held joint religious and socialist objections. The remaining 30 per cent cited a variety of reasons for their conscientious objection.)

War and Resistance

Rotoaira Prison Camp

Under the provisions of the Expeditionary Forces Amendment Act, military defaulters were deprived of their civil rights for ten years from 10 December 1918. This included the right to work for the Crown or any other local or public authority, including teaching; the right to be elected or appointed to serve as a Member of Parliament or on any other local or public authority; and the right to be enrolled to vote in elections for Members of Parliament or any other local or public authority. Defaulters who were overseas at the time the Act was passed were prohibited from returning to New Zealand for ten years; if they returned they would be subject to deportation. Any attempted breach of the Act attracted, upon conviction, up to twelve months in prison.

The disqualification expired on 10 December 1928. There was a proposal to remove the disability one year sooner, when the Government introduced the War Disabilities Removal Bill in September 1927, but the Legislative Council (the Upper House) cut out that provision.[18] Managers were appointed from each Chamber to hold a conference in an attempt to resolve the impasse. The managers failed to come to a decision. The Legislative Council managers included Sir Robert Stout (1844-1930),

Chapter 3

John A. Lee

the former Prime Minister and Chief Justice who had previously been known as a supporter of labour rights and social reform, but was not liberal on this issue. Managers for the House of Representatives (the Lower House) included John A. Lee (1891-1982), member for Auckland East. A wounded and highly decorated war veteran, Lee would later become the *enfant terrible* of the Labour government. Divisions over conscientious objectors and the war were still deeply felt at the war's end as John A. Lee stated:

> It just shows how hard hatred really dies. Disqualifications of the nature proposed in the clause had been wiped off the Statue Book in other countries and men who had been disqualified in Great Britain were now members of Parliament.[19]

John A. Lee said that he trusted the Prime Minister would reinstate the clause in the next session. The Prime Minister, Gordon Coates (1878-1943), agreed to accept the Legislative Council's amendment and not insist on retaining the clause which lifted restrictions on conscientious objectors so that the rest of the Bill could be saved. The Prime Minister stated that he thought all feelings of bitterness aroused by the war should be wiped out. He regretted what the Legislative Council had done and hoped that next year they would take a more humane and reasonable view. However, there was no further attempt to modify the ten-year loss of civil rights.[20]

Return to Society: Tutoring and Political Activity

The Great War ended on 11 November 1918. However, Norman Murray Bell, like other defaulters, had to serve his full term of imprisonment, and was not released until five months after the armistice ended the war. On release he returned to his parents' house at 134 Fitzgerald Street, St Albans, Christchurch,[21] where he lived for the remainder of his life. The house remained unchanged throughout his lifetime, though he was joined by his spinster sister Winifred and for a long period of time they lived there together. Being barred from so many positions that involved government-related work, Norman Murray Bell resumed providing private tuition. Within a week, his first newspaper advertisement appeared saying he had resumed coaching at Fitzgerald Street, St Albans.[22] For the next seventeen years, he provided individual tuition to University Entrance examination students in a wide range of subjects, including Classics and Analytical Chemistry in a private laboratory in his home.

In 1919, Norman Murray Bell was appointed Tutor in Sociology by the Workers' Educational Association of Canterbury (CWEA).[23] He would be reappointed many times to tutor courses at the CWEA: in international relations in 1930, Esperanto in 1933, New Zealand's cultural and political development in 1936. In addition, the CWEA began a series of "air lectures" on Radio 3YA in 1931. CWEA tutors, including Norman Murray Bell, provided 25-minute talks, which the tutors had a free hand in preparing. Although political questions were not encouraged, the CWEA tutors usually went to the radio studio and read their prepared scripts live without having to obtain prior approval. However, in 1933 one of the tutors was cut off air by the station manager because of the political viewpoint he expressed. The New Zealand Broadcasting Board then required the CWEA to submit its list of talks before broadcast for approval. When the Board requested the script of Norman Murray Bell's talk on the Samoan mandate, which New Zealand received from the League of Nations, his proposed talk was rejected by the Board. New Zealand's recent history included the shooting of Samoan protestors by New Zealand police in 1929, and Norman Murray Bell was an advocate for Samoan independence. Such topics were politically unacceptable. In its place he substituted an innocuous talk concerning the idea of progress. In 1931, Norman Murray

Chapter 3

Bell spoke on air about Esperanto; the following year, at the fourth New Zealand Esperanto Congress, he was elected a Vice President.

Shortly after his return home, Norman Murray Bell began political lobbying under the auspices of the Conscientious Objectors Fellowship. This fellowship had been formed with the object of fighting militarism. Its advocates believed that freedom of conscience was the foundation of political and individual freedom. Meetings were held in the Trades and Labour Hall, where, with the Methodist minister Rev. Percy N. Knight (1867-1944), he protested against the jailing of conscientious objectors, and called for those imprisoned to be released. Letters on the same subject were written to newspapers. The movement also opposed conscription.

Norman Murray Bell was a frequent contributor to the *Maoriland Worker*, having been introduced to the editor by Charles Mackie (1869-1943). Mackie had founded the National Peace Council in 1911. A former Missionary-Organiser for the New Zealand Baptist Union, Mackie was leader of the Canterbury Baptist Lay Preachers Association, which opposed militarism, calling for passive resistance against laws which conflicted with Christian principles. He became disenchanted with the church's support of militarism.

The paper was a co-defendant in the only New Zealand case for blasphemous libel when, together with its publisher John Glover (1866-1947), it was prosecuted in 1922 for publishing Siegfried Sassoon's war poem "Stand To: Good Friday Morning" on the front page of the 12 October 1921 edition:

> I'd been on duty from two till four.
> I went and stared at the dug-out door.
> Down in the frost I heard them snore.
> 'Stand to!' Somebody grunted and swore.
> Dawn was misty; the skies were still;
> Larks were singing, discordant, shrill;
> *They* seemed happy; but *I* felt ill.
> Deep in water I splashed my way
> Up the trench to our bogged front line.
> Rain had fallen the whole damned night.
> O Jesus, send me a wound to-day,
> And I'll believe in Your bread and wine,
> And get my bloody old sins washed white!

The jury found Glover and the newspaper not guilty, but added a rider to the effect that they wished to see similar publications discouraged. Was their rider tongue-in-cheek, given that the decision they had just rendered made further publications more rather than less likely, or was it simply naivety? The blasphemy trial for this war poem was incongruous; the poem reflected the views held by many soldiers, as well as pacifists and other conscientious objectors, that the mainstream churches had supported the World War with its attendant destruction of human life. Those who faced the consequences of such religious endorsement of killing were surely entitled to point out, even in an irreverent way, how much they wanted to avoid death.

It was a short step from Norman Murray Bell's political activity to joining the New Zealand Labour Party, which had been formed in 1916 out of several left-wing parties and trade unions. Christchurch had been the radical centre of the old Liberal Party and became of considerable significance to the new Labour movement. In addition to the progressive political organisations that were swept into the new Labour Party, Christchurch was the home of ardent anti-militarism. This was the result of the New Zealand government's decision in 1909 to donate to England a state-of-the-art battleship costing £2 million, and also the introduction of compulsory military training. "For some, militarism was opposed as one of the oppressive outgrowths of capitalism; for others, simple humanitarian grounds were more important; some simply opposed compulsion."[24] The anti-militarist advocacy provided an even greater impetus to the new political movement.

In 1919 Norman Murray Bell was nominated by the Christchurch North branch of the New Zealand Labour Party for the forthcoming general election. However, as a result of being placed on the Defaulters List, he was unable to stand, and his nomination was withdrawn. In 1923, at the Labour Party's conference, Bell was unsuccessfully nominated for the position of Vice President. But this was just the beginning of his political life. On 9 June 1919, he was invited by Charles Mackie to join the National Peace Council of New Zealand. Three days later Norman Murray Bell wrote accepting the invitation which he felt "honoured" by receiving and promised to do whatever he could to further "the cause of universal peace." The two men had previously corresponded before and during the time Norman Murray Bell was imprisoned in Rotoaira prison.[25]

4

Working for Peace

Movements Against War and Fascism, 1921-1939

The No More War Movement and Other Anti-War Organizations

The No More War international movement was founded in Britain in 1921. The movement received messages of support from several international figures, including Albert Einstein. In 1923, the British movement inspired a No More War public rally in Christchurch which was addressed by Bob Semple (1873-1955), a well-known Labour spokesman who had been imprisoned during the Great War for his anti-war activities. The Christchurch No More War meeting was organised by a joint committee of the Labour Party and the National Peace Council. The chairman, the Rev. Percy Paris (1882-1942), a Methodist minister with a radical pacifist and socialist vision of Christianity that included support for the development of a welfare state, paid tribute to those who had fallen in the last war, and those who had refused to fight for the sake of their conscience. He then read the following resolution: "That the time has come to demand that governments of the world disarm completely by mutual agreement." This was carried unanimously. Bob Semple closed the meeting by urging people to join the National Peace Council. Norman Murray Bell wrote an account of this rally in the *Maoriland Worker*.[1]

The 1923 rally did not attempt to form a new organisation. The New Zealand No More War Movement, committed to absolute pacifism, was founded in 1928 by Alfred ("Fred") Page (1899-1930), together with Lincoln Efford (1907-1962). Fred Page had been educated at Christchurch Boys High, and was a student during the time Norman Murray Bell taught there. He won university scholarships and attended Canterbury University College, gaining a Master of Arts degree with First Class Honours in botany. His father was a lecturer in chemistry at the university college, and his mother, also an active pacifist, had been headmistress of a girls' school. After the war, Fred Page became a teacher at the Socialist Sunday School, where he founded a weekly newspaper called *The Sunbeam*. He returned to Christchurch Boys High in 1920 as an assistant teacher; however, he was dismissed in 1922 when he refused to sign the teachers' oath of allegiance unless it included a conscience clause. He then began spending more time in anti-war work. In 1930, he went to Europe to attend a conference of the War Resisters International. Tragically, he died on his first night in Paris from a gas leak while a guest in the home of an English Quaker.

Lincoln Efford had grown up in the Socialist Sunday School, which introduced him to pacifism. In 1920 he attended the first summer school of the Workers' Educational Association. He was a strong supporter of

The No More War Committee, c. 1930
Norman Bell (seated centre) holds photo of the late Fred Page.
Sarah Page is seated on Bell's left.
Back row: Lincoln Efford (far right); Charles Mackie (second from right).

Chapter 4

Third New Zealand Esperanto Conference, Christchurch, 1931
Front row: Lincoln Efford (second from left); Norman Murray Bell (far right).

the Labour Party and member of the New Zealand Esperanto Association, serving as secretary-treasurer of the Christchurch branch. He was a member of the Peace Pledge Union for many years, and after the outbreak of World War II he helped organised the Combined Pacifist Committee. During the war he established the Co-operative Press in a room off Chancery Lane in Christchurch. (The Lane was located off Gloucester Street and emerged into Cathedral Square. Number 30 Chancery Lane was the meeting place for a number of peace organisations over many years, and home for the Free Religious Movement until 1944.)

Auckland, the largest city in the country, had very limited peace-movement organisation before the outbreak of war. In June 1913, the New Zealand Freedom League was formed, comprised mostly of Quakers and Unitarians. The first chairman, Rev. Richard Hall (1883-1930), minister of the Auckland Unitarian Church, assisted compulsory military-training dissenters to apply for exemption from the Courts, produced anti-war leaflets, and was active in advocating the peace viewpoint in newspapers and to politicians. Hall left New Zealand at the end of 1913 to take charge of a church in South Africa; by November 1914

Working for Peace

Chancery Lane, Christchurch, 1932

this peace organisation had become inactive. This was the same year the Student Christian Movement, at its inaugural conference in the country town of Woodville in the lower North Island, was addressed by the American Quaker John Fletcher, who strongly advocated pacifism. His address would have a lasting effect as the organisation embraced pacifism and influenced generations of members to come.[2] Many members became active pacifists during the 1930s. One such was Lloyd Geering, who recorded: "What soon came to influence me even more than my association with First Church, Dunedin, was the Student Christian Movement…" and "I for one remained a pacifist when World War II broke out because I had in 1937 embraced the Christian faith along with the way of life that I fervently believed it entailed." When he entered the ministry he "found many of my fellow divinity students were already pacifist."[3] Later Lloyd Geering would rise to prominence as Principal of Knox Theological Hall, during the years 1963 to 1971.

Chapter 4

Unlike Auckland, Christchurch had a strong peace movement before the war. Early office-holders of the No More War Movement included Charles Mackie.[4] Harry Albert Atkinson (1867-1956), who had worked in the Labour Church Movement in Britain, was an original member of the Peace Council.

Other leading office-holders in the No More War Movement were Norman Murray Bell, its first chairman, and the Rev. Clyde Carr (1886-1962), a radical minister and ardent advocate of the social gospel, who became the longest-serving Labour MP. Pastor Charles Henry Cole (1894-1962) became the No More War Movement's organising secretary and first full-time office-holder in 1929.[5] Charles Cole arrived at St Albans Baptist Church when it opened in 1926 with his wife Kathleen Hilda (née Clemens; they would separate in 1930 and later divorce). He served as a Baptist home missionary,[6] undertaking the course of study laid down by the Baptist College committee. He was involved in a children's and young people's ministry, became editor of the church magazine *Christian Manhood* and served as president of the Canterbury District of the New Zealand Baptist Unions. Born in England, where his parents were still living, he had immigrated to New Zealand and during the war served in the New Zealand Army Medical Corps.[7] He reacted with intense feeling that war was utterly un-Christian and he was passionate in the fight for universal peace.[8] Previously he had been involved in the Canterbury Unemployed Workers Association; he resigned from St Albans church in 1929 to work for the No More War Movement — clearly the right man for the job.

At the second Annual Meeting of the Movement, Norman Murray Bell was elected chairman, and the Rev. Clyde Carr vice-chairman. An important address was given that year by Lilian Edger (1862-1941) on "Pathways to World Peace". Miss Edger, well known for her exceptional public speaking style, was a daughter of the Rev. Samuel Edger, who had been minister to the Albertland settlers and was an ardent pacifist. She was one of the first New Zealand women to obtain a university degree. A major achievement by the Movement in 1930 was the petition organised by the Rev. Charles Cole to repeal sections of the Defence Act. By December 1931, some 15,000 signatures were obtained, an impressive result. This was influential in the government's decision to suspend the compulsory military training sections of the Defence Act.

Working for Peace

The first Dominion Conference of the No More War Movement was held in Christchurch on 5 January 1931. It was chaired by Norman Murray Bell as president. Bell had now found his metier, having entered the national stage as a leading peace advocate. Delegates were sent from branches in all the main centres. The conference passed resolutions seeking confirmation from the government that military training in schools was on a "purely voluntary basis", and supporting calls for Samoan independence. The Movement also organised an essay competition for Christchurch schoolchildren on the Kellogg-Briand Pact; the mayor of Christchurch, Daniel Sullivan (1882-1947), presented the banner and competition prizes won by pupils of the West Christchurch District High School. The Kellogg-Briand Pact had been devised in 1928 by the American Secretary of State, Frank Kellogg, and the French Foreign Minister, Aristide Briand, providing for nations to renounce the use of war as an instrument of policy towards each other. By the time it came into effect in 1929 it had been signed by 62 countries; that year Frank Kellogg received the Nobel Peace Prize for his work on the Pact, Briand having received the same award in 1926. Until then international law had given countries the right to wage war for conquest: now this was outlawed. The significance of the Pact at first appeared to be in the idealism it expressed for peace. However, more recent analysis has argued that it succeeded in reducing the frequency of worldwide territorial conquest from an average of one incident every ten months to one every four years.[9]

West Christchurch District High School
Ensom Essay competition winners with the Mayor with the Headmaster.

Chapter 4

Frank B. Kellogg and Aristide Briand

By 1932, the Movement had been re-organised into a national New Zealand No More War Movement. Norman Murray Bell was chairman and Sarah Page secretary. The Movement urged the New Zealand government to act under the mandate of the League of Nations to oppose Japanese aggression in Manchuria. They affiliated with the War Resisters' International movement, a growing worldwide organisation advocating world peace. Contacts were forged with the National Peace Council, Trades and Labour Council, Women's Christian Temperance Union, Labour Party, League of Nations Union, Student Christian Movement, the Workers' Educational Association, and the Friends of the Soviet Union. The movement wrote to the prime minister seeking support for the League of Nations' proposal to add a clause to the Kellogg-Briand Peace Pact pledging complete disarmament of all countries.

At the annual conference of the No More War Movement in January 1934, mayor Daniel Sullivan observed: "It may have been said before the Great War, that Europe was an armed camp, it is even more true to say it today." His words reflected the heightened tension amongst nations, as delegates had to face up to the increasing threat to world peace. The principal speaker was Frederick Sinclaire, Professor of English Literature at Canterbury University College. He expressed pessimism about the state of higher education concerning world affairs. He wondered how many university students were knowledgeable about current events in Russia, Japan, Italy and Germany (in other words, the totalitarian states).

Working for Peace

Frederick and Esther Sinclaire

He thought many of them were hopelessly ignorant. Norman Murray Bell spoke in defence of freedom to use the radio "for the broadcasting of as much controversial matter as possible." (His passion for the public purpose in accessing radio was shown in an article he wrote in *Tomorrow* arguing that "vital problems of the day" should be aired from "opposing points of view" and this would allow democratic use of "one of the most powerful educative instruments of our day."[10]) Addresses were also given by representatives of the Workers' Educational Association and the League of Nations Union. The conference concluded with a garden party at the family home of Mrs Sarah Page.

Ties were maintained between the No More War Movement and the War Resisters' International with the nomination by the New Zealand No More War Movement of James Saunders to the council of the War Resisters' International; Saunders also represented the New Zealand movement at the international peace conference in Holland in July 1934. That year the No More War Movement supervised the Ensom Peace Prize contest amongst Christchurch schools. This would become an annual event for the Movement. The Prize, established in 1931 by a bequest from Sarah Ann Ensom (c. 1840-1929), took the form of an essay competition on international peace and goodwill. (Another Ensom Prize was awarded for the successful student peace essay at Canterbury University College.) Sarah Ensom and her husband William Ensom (1852-1923) were long-standing supporters of the National Peace Council.

Chapter 4

The seventh annual Dominion conference of the New Zealand No More War Movement commenced in January 1935; as before, a garden party was held at the home of Sarah Page in Christchurch. The conference got underway with delegates from Wellington, Napier, Dunedin and Christchurch. Noticeably absent was Auckland, the largest city, as no branch was organised there. The president, Norman Murray Bell, opened the business with a call for Samoan self-government. The principal speaker was Rev. Charles Cole, who addressed the conference on the need for collective resistance to war. The proposal he presented involved calling a general strike and refusing to take part in military service to frustrate attempts to start a war. Another suggestion was to have an act passed by Parliament that required a referendum before conscription could be introduced. A reaction to the heightened risk of war can be seen in the proposal from the National Peace Council, which was presented to the No More War Movement in May 1935 by Harry Atkinson. This idea would have declared New Zealand a demilitarised zone under international convention carried out with the authority of the League of Nations. This convention would ensure that no vessels or warplanes would be allowed within one thousand miles of the Dominion. Under this proposal, all armaments and military training in New Zealand would be prohibited.

The annual conference of the No More War Movement in January 1936 began with another garden party at the residence of Mrs Sarah Page, where delegates were welcomed by Daniel Sullivan, the mayor of Christchurch. Congratulations were sent to two Dunedin members of the Movement, Messrs Archie Campbell (1874-1955) and Peter Neilson (1879-1948), upon their election as Labour Party members of parliament. Addresses were given by Mr H. Winston Rhodes (1905-1987) on economic sanctions and ethics. He advocated "an ethical code of life affirmation such as held by Dr Schweitzer".[11] He thought imperialism was unethical and fascism was cultural barbarism. While he was sympathetic to the suffering of the Italian people under fascism, he opposed Italian intervention in Abyssinia. James Saunders, the overseas representative of the Movement, spoke on the war and peace situation. He urged the government through the League of Nations to produce a practical scheme of general disarmament. He reaffirmed the movement's attitude of absolute pacifism and opposition to Italian aggression in Abyssinia. (In 1935 James Saunders had been unanimously elected chairman of the Dunedin Branch of the No More War Movement.)

Norman Murray Bell was re-elected national president of the No More War Movement and Millicent Baxter (née Brown, 1888-1984), wife of Archibald Baxter (1881-1979), the well-known Dunedin pacifist, was elected as vice president. Archibald Baxter, a committed pacifist and Christian socialist, was the founder of the Dunedin branch of the No More War Movement in 1930. During World War I, following the denial of his application for conscientious objector status, he was inducted into the New Zealand army and forcibly transported to France, where he was tied in a cross position at the front exposed to enemy fire. In 1939 Archibald Baxter wrote about his wartime experiences in *We Will Not Cease*.[12]

There appear to have been no further No More War Movement Dominion conferences after 1936. The year was a watershed for the peace movements, as the weakness of the League of Nations became more apparent and newer, more vital pacifist organisations emerged.

New religiously-based peace initiatives emerged in the mid-1930s: a Fellowship of Pacifist Ministers attracted clergy in Canterbury and Westland from the Church of England, Presbyterian, Methodist, Baptist and Congregationalist churches. Members refused to be associated in any way with war, including the preparation for war; to bear arms or encourage anyone else to bear arms; to give moral support for war, or to take the military oath. They supported the work of the League of Nations in its efforts encouraging international co-operation. They described war as the denial of "the brotherhood and love at which the Gospel of Christ calls all men to aim."[13]

The Christian Pacifist Society was formed in Wellington in 1936 by Ormond Burton (1893-1974), a Methodist minister and veteran of the Great War, and lay preacher Archibald Barrington (1906-1986).[14] This was followed by the Peace Pledge Union in Christchurch in 1938, founded by Thurlow and Kathleen Thompson, who had immigrated to New Zealand. Thurlow, a prominent Anglican layman, was editor of the Christchurch diocesan magazine, and Kathleen became publicity officer for the Peace Pledge Union, which had been founded in Britain

Chapter 4

by the Rev. Dick Sheppard (1880-1937) four years earlier. It would soon spread to other towns in the North Island.[15] Now highly motivated, the Women's International League for Peace and Freedom re-emerged in Auckland and started organising a national petition for unconditional disarmament in 1932. The New Zealand petition became part of an international petition of some eight million signatures presented to the League of Nations disarmament conference in Geneva in 1933. That year Germany withdrew from the League of Nations; the disarmament conference failed.

The events of the Spanish Civil War, which began in July 1936 with the military coup against the elected Republican government, greatly affected the anti-war peace movement in New Zealand. It was a turning point in foreign policy relations between New Zealand and Britain: for the first time New Zealand defied the home country, with its independent and outspoken support for the constitutional Spanish republican government.[16]

The rise of Hitler provoked yet another international peace response, including the formation of the Movement Against War and Fascism, which first appeared in Auckland in 1934. It soon spread to Wellington, Christchurch and Dunedin, holding its first congress in Wellington the same year. The second congress held in 1935 was an impressive affair: 60 delegates from 46 organisations attended, including trade unions, the Women's League for International Peace and Freedom, churches and laypeople. The national secretary was Gerald Griffin (1904-1976), a trade union activist. In 1936 the Movement Against War and Fascism advocated a complete cessation of the Spanish civil war. However, the new Labour Government refused to allow its members to join the Movement Against War and Fascism, and it barely survived 1937.

The No More War Movement, still headed by Norman Murray Bell, joined other peace organisations in publicly opposing the fascist-supported aggression in Spain, the invasion of Abyssinia by Italy and Japan's invasion of Manchuria. By August 1939, great consternation was felt in the peace movements regarding the approaching war in Western Europe. Part of their response was a proposal that New Zealand should remain neutral in the developing conflict between Germany, France, and Britain. As pacifist support grew it received a rebuke from the Labour Prime Minister Michael Savage (1872-1940), who said that its

Working for Peace

Peace March, c.1937

members were dreamers, cranks and ideological oddities. While this may have seemed incongruous coming from a Labour leader, many of whose colleagues had gone to prison for their opposition to the Great War, it was delivered shortly after war broke out and, unbeknown to the public, the Prime Minister was dying.

Bloomsbury South

By now there was a noticeable activity in peace advocacy among the intellectual, literary and artistic groups located in Christchurch. From 1933 to 1953 New Zealand experienced a blossoming in literary creation, poetry and prose, printing and publishing, painting and theatre production and music. This movement was largely centred in Christchurch. Because of the parallels between the earlier English Bloomsbury group and that of Christchurch, the later has been identified as "Bloomsbury South" in the seminal work *Bloomsbury South: The Arts in Christchurch 1933-1953*.[17]

Bloomsbury South comprised three overlapping circles of artists and intellectuals, who within the confines of this southern city were well known to each other. One gathered around the poet and Anglican

Chapter 4

Ursula Bethell

social worker Ursula Bethell (1874-1945), frequenting her home, Rise Cottage, in the Cashmere Hills with its views over the Southern Alps and the Canterbury Plains. Members of this circle included the editor and novelist Monte Holcroft (1902-1993), the composer Douglas Lilburn (1915-2001), the poet, literary editor and arts patron Charles Brasch (1909-1973), the painter Toss Woollaston (1910-1998), the poet and writer D'Arcy Cresswell (1896-1960), and poets Denis Glover (1912-1980) and Allen Curnow (1911-2001). Ursula Bethell became a mentor to many of these younger people, advising on their professional development. (In 1979 the Ursula Bethell Residency in Creative Writing was established at the University of Canterbury, jointly funded by the Canterbury College of Arts and Creative New Zealand.)

A second circle gathered around the Caxton Press,[18] which had been founded by the poet Denis Glover. The Caxton Press, which had begun life as a university club in 1932, served much the same function as did the Hogarth Press in London: it mainly published the poets and writers of Bloomsbury South, often in small runs with bespoke typography. It also published theatre programmes for Shakespearean productions by Ngaio Marsh (1895-1982) a leading theatre director and crime writer of international repute.

Working for Peace

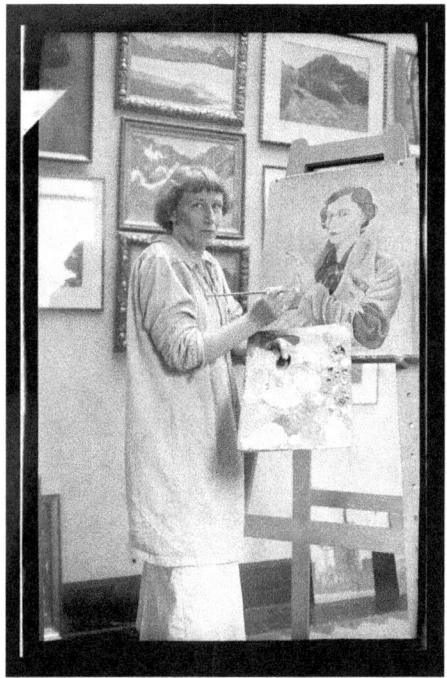

Rita Angus painting self portrait, 1936-1937

The third circle was The Group, which had been formed as an exhibiting society of younger women artists in 1927.¹⁹ The painter Rita Angus (1908-1970) was among its original members. In 1935 she had a tiny studio in Chancery Lane. Late in 1936, she moved into a studio flat at 97a Cambridge Terrace, and in 1938, as The Group was broadened, she was joined in the adjoining flat 97b by the painter Leo Bensemann (1912-1986) and Caxton Press editor and writer Lawrence Baigent (1912-1985). Allen Curnow and his wife Betty (1911-2005) a painter and printmaker, were frequent visitors.²⁰ Douglas Lilburn lived nearby at 175 Cambridge Terrace, beside the Avon River.

Most members of Bloomsbury South were pacifists and supported the peace cause at a time of increasing militarism. The election of the first Labour government in 1935 laid the foundations for the modern welfare state and introduced Keynesian economic management to deal with the distress caused by the Great Depression. Prime Minister Savage called his policies applied Christianity; his conservative detractors called

Chapter 4

*Cambridge Terrace apartments, by the Avon River
Douglas Lilburn lived at No 175. Rita Angus and others nearby in two
studio flats at No 97, where artists, writers, poets and musicians met.
The buildings were demolished for the Christchurch Town Hall complex.*

it applied lunacy. History has shown that the Prime Minister was right. It was seen as a time of political renewal and hope by the majority of New Zealanders.

In the late 1930s the major issue facing the Bloomsbury South group was the drumbeat of war in Europe and Asia. A number of the members joined one or more of the peace movements on offer. Some expressed their views in articles in the publication *Tomorrow*, founded and edited by Andrew Kennaway Henderson (1879-1960), published from 1934 to 1940 and aimed at a politically aware readership. Henderson was a humanitarian socialist who had been twice imprisoned during the Great War as a conscientious objector. He was supported in this endeavour by Professor Frederick Sinclaire and H. Winston Rhodes, then a lecturer in English at Canterbury University College, who were on the editorial board of *Tomorrow* from the beginning. They were later joined by Denis Glover. For a while Glover was assisted at the Caxton Press by an old school friend, Bob Lowry (1912-1963), an accomplished printer

Working for Peace

Ian Milner, Denis Glover and Robert Lowry, Christchurch, 1933

and publisher who moved south when he ran into problems with the administration at Auckland University College.

The Bloomsbury South authors followed in the footsteps of many earlier writers, from the Jewish and Christian scriptures (Isaiah 2:4: "They shall beat their swords into ploughshares..."; Matthew 5:1-12: "Blessed are the peacemakers: for they shall be called the children of God") to pacifist Humanist writings. "Either man must abolish war, or war will abolish man," wrote Bertrand Russell in 1915; and as R.S. White expressed it in *Pacifism and English Literature*, "Peaceful living, rather than violent killing, is the basis for rational pacifism, and it is self-evidently violated by war."[21] In England, as Hitler annexed Austria, Virginia Woolf published her polemic *Three Guineas*, written as three letters seeking support for an anti-war society, a fund for women's education and support for women in the professions. It has been described as "an artful but vehement critique of the ties that bind patriarchy and fascism, men's appetite for war ... and the march toward battlefield graves."[22]

In New Zealand, Allen Curnow, after completing his theological training, decided in 1934 he could not join the Anglican clergy. He subsequently became a major twentieth-century poet. With the outbreak of war, he wrote a significant twenty-year review of English poetry entitled "Prophets of Their Time: Some Modern Poets".[23] Reviewing the works of T.S. Eliot, W. H. Auden, Cecil Day-Lewis, Stephen Spender, David Gascoyne and W. B. Yeats, Curnow argued that before the Great War "the prophetic spirit was noticeably absent from English poetry, just as the last 20 years have been notable for its ... re-appearance." A survey of poetry in the last twenty years, he argued, is "filled with warnings of impending disasters, with bitter indignation against human wrongs. There is something of the vision of Isaiah: 'The earth mourneth and fadeth away, the world languisheth and fadeth away, the lofty people of the earth do languish.'" He saw affinities between the words of modern poets and those of Isaiah and the Minor Prophets, although each of the Old Testament prophecies bore "the stamp of its own age; it is couched in the terms of its own particular epoch; it is shaped to meet the special needs of those to whom it was first addressed ..." When poetry foresees that something is going to happen — in this case, war on a horrific world scale — "at such times the authentic voice of prophecy is heard." Prophecy springs from the compulsion to address the nation and the human race, and in these circumstances poetry is really speaking with authority. "If that is so, prophecy should be poetry at its highest ..." The Curnow article, written just three months after the outbreak of war, was a tour de force describing the place and importance of poetry in contemporary society.

European refugees, often Jewish, fleeing from fascism, such as the Austrian born philosopher Karl Popper (1902-1994), author of *The Open Society and Its Enemies*, began settling in Christchurch. They would provide further intellectual, artistic and musical stimuli in Christchurch.[24]

Old Religion into New: The Free Religious Movement

The origins of the Free Religious Movement in New Zealand grew out of the church founded by Rev. James Chapple (1865-1947). Due to his opposition to World War I, Chapple left New Zealand for America in July 1915 with his wife Florence and thirteen of their fourteen children. The eldest son, Leonard (1893-1980), a school teacher, enlisted in the Auckland Regiment in 1916 in opposition to his parents' pacifist beliefs.

Working for Peace

James Chapple

At the end of the war, he held the rank of Lieutenant and remained in voluntary service after the war as a Captain in the Territorial Forces (now the Reserve Forces). Leonard gave his father's address on his Army record as Nottingham Avenue (now Santa Barbara Road), Thousand Oaks, Berkeley, California. Although James Chapple could have had a ministerial position on the Pacific coast, he spent all his time engaged in anti-war work, promoting the ideals of social justice which merged into socialism, and making many friends within these movements.[25] The Chapple family returned to New Zealand at the end of 1916, before America entered the war, because the two youngest children were homesick. Four children remained in America and a fifth returned later to marry her fiancé.

Capitalising on the nascent activity that had been undertaken in his absence, in particular by Edward McDonnell (1862-1945), an Australian lay leader from his old church at Timaru, Chapple was able to start a Unitarian Church in Christchurch with the ground well prepared. Originally he and his wife Florence were Salvation Army officers from Australia; James Chapple became an ordained Presbyterian minister in 1903 and had charge of St Andrews Church, South Canterbury. Because of his support from the pulpit for the working class, the Presbytery tried to remove him but failed in the face of the overwhelming support he received from his parishioners. Then the Presbytery sought to begin an inquiry after Chapple chaired a public meeting for the noted English ex-Catholic priest, Joseph McCabe (1867-1955). At the Presbytery meeting, Chapple read a letter of explanation and then resigned from the church, saving it the trouble of an inquiry. Any remaining doubt about his heterodoxy was extinguished when he opened a Unitarian church in Timaru in 1912.

The Unitarian Church had begun services in 1916 using the Christchurch Masonic Hall before his return, and Chapple continued using the same venue throughout his ministry. In 1917 Chapple went on a speaking tour against the war. In March 1918 he was charged with sedition, and in May sentenced to 11 months imprisonment with hard labour. The words that got him into trouble were:

> You are under the heels of the war lords. We have not enough population for our own country, yet we are lusting after the annexation of Samoa. The patriotic poison is in our schools. Children are taught to salute the flag and taught to sing the National Anthem. I tell my children, when they come home, not to sing the National Anthem. I am hoping with a fervent hope that in this war there will be no victor to pray about. A war is blasphemy. A woman goes down the valley of death to bring a child into the world, she nurses it, sends it to school, sees it through the sixth standards, and then comes the call to arms, and it goes away to war. What for? To die for its country? No; to die for the profiteer.
>
> [...] Russia wanted war, England wanted war, the upper class in New Zealand wanted war. Never has there been such a wonderful five days [meaning the days of the Russian revolution]. The old Russia has gone and the new Russia has come in. I hope before I die to see a similar movement in New Zealand. I hope the day will come in New Zealand when these war lords will be repudiated. I hope not a penny of the war loan will be repaid. You do not authorise them.[26]

He also stated his criticism of the mainstream churches, saying, "If Jesus Christ was now on earth he would be tried for sedition. The churches are the recruiting agent for the world's greatest tragedies."

After eight months Chapple was given early release from Paparoa Prison in January 1919. While there he had been protected from the worst demands of manual work by his fellow prisoners, who took care of the middle-aged parson and friend of the working class. After his

Working for Peace

release Chapple returned to his Christchurch church. In his absence, the church had been kept going by visits from speakers from his old church at Timaru, aided by visiting Unitarian ministers from Wellington and Auckland. His church organised a large "welcome home" party at the Trades Hall on the Saturday evening of his release.

During 1918, the Christchurch church Sunday school was renamed the Socialist Sunday School, with 120 children on the roll. This was the beginning of the radicalization of the church, which was to occur over the next decade. The new Sunday school membership card stated, "We desire to be just and loving to all men and women; to work together as brothers and sisters; to be kind to every living creature, and to help to form a new society with justice as its foundation and love as its law."

At this stage, Norman Murray Bell was a teacher at the Socialist Sunday School along with Fred Page. From 1923, they edited the *International Sunbeam* magazine, which became a quarterly publication for the Sunday school children. It attracted controversy from those opposed to the idea of Socialist Sunday school, mainly because it was not providing Bible teaching. However the Anglican Archdeacon of Christchurch, the Rev. Percy Bolton Haggitt (1878-1957), who served in the diocese from 1918 to 1934, said of the magazine: "If you read the *International Sunbeam* ... there is a ring of earnestness about it — that

Socialist Sunday School wagon trip, Auckland, 1920s

Chapter 4

is what struck me — and there is real Christianity in it and a great deal of misunderstanding as to what the Church stands for."[27] In 1920 the Christchurch Socialist Sunday School founded a choir, which was followed in 1921 when the Auckland Socialist Sunday School formed the Sunbeams Socialist Choir. At the No More War rally in Christchurch in 1923, children from the Socialist Sunday School performed a play voicing their aspirations for a better world.

James Chapple undertook an expansion of this movement, based on the model that had been earlier developed in Britain; and he had also seen the Socialist Sunday School at Oakland, California, the first of its kind, on the Pacific coast during his visit in 1915-16. He wrote a number of articles promoting Socialist Sunday schools in the *Maoriland Worker*. By 1920 Palmerston North had a Socialist Sunday school; by 1921 one had started in Auckland and the following year in Wellington and Dunedin. The Socialist Sunday Schools taught science subjects, provided lectures on astronomy and evolution. In Palmerston North, Esperanto was encouraged. The children played outside games where possible, such as cricket, rounders, tennis, and boating.

The modern Socialist Sunday Schools grew out of international movements at the beginning of the twentieth century; some were Christian socialists who had founded the Labour Church and others were ethical socialists with or without church affiliation. The Socialist Sunday School movement developed in Britain, Belgium, Hungary, Switzerland, Canada, and Australia. The organisation of the schools were often modelled along mainstream church lines: students recited ten socialist principles, sang socialist hymns, and learnt about great men and women who had worked for the good of humanity.[28]

Not everyone was sanguine about the arrival of Socialist Sunday Schools in this small dominion of the British Empire. The Sunday Schools were accused of engaging in "godless propaganda" from which all Bible teaching was eliminated; a 1922 editorial in the *Star* claimed that these Sunday Schools were "a very serious menace to the Empire" and "a direct challenge to the very foundations of civilisation." The editorial ended by saying, "we see no reason whatsoever why the Socialist Sunday schools should not be rigidly suppressed."[29] However, the extreme condemnation of the Socialist Sunday Schools caused an unexpected reaction. Mrs Leech from Dunedin was attending the

1923 Conference of the National Council of Women in Auckland when allegations were made about the irreligious nature of the Socialist Sunday Schools. She took the opportunity to investigate the teachings of the Socialist Sunday School in Auckland. Mrs Leech said she was very pleased because the teaching "contains nothing pernicious and is perfectly free from any revolutionary or un-Christian doctrine." She added, "I have seen the hymn book used in the Auckland Sunday School, and I can only admire the beautiful ethics and love and community fellowship expressed therein."[30]

By now, James Chapple was the superintendent of the Internationalist Socialist School in Christchurch, and Norman Murray Bell deputy superintendent. However, James Chapple now felt confident that the church leadership was strong enough for him to be absent for periods, allowing him to travel overseas. His first visit was back to San Francisco in 1920, where he met up with members of his family who had settled in the United States. This was followed by a trip in 1923 to Australia, visiting Sydney and Brisbane, where he gave an address in the Trades Hall denouncing Capitalism, Nationalism and Imperialism as a menace to human progress.

His next trip was further afield: he went to Britain in April 1924. His principal reason for going was to meet his publisher, Charles William Daniel (1871-1955), whose imprint, the C.W. Daniel Company in London, had published Chapple's *The Divine Need of the Rebel* in February 1924. This book was based on his lectures delivered at the church services held in the Masonic Hall in Christchurch. Daniel's publishing house specialised in publishing books about pacifism, food reform, and alternative medicine. They also published works by Walter Walsh, leader of the Free Religious Movement in Britain whose ministry only had five years to run. He promoted a multi-faith approach, seeking the best ethical principles he found in each of the major world religions. During the Great War, Daniel was twice prosecuted for works he had published. The first was his own *The Knock-Out Blow*, an attack on Britain's war policy. The second, *Despised and Rejected*, was a novel by Rose Allatini with themes of homosexuality and pacifism. When Daniel was fined and refused to pay, he was imprisoned. (In recent years the company was taken over by Random House.)

Chapter 4

While in Britain, Chapple travelled to the Lake District, where he wrote that "some of the most beautiful days on my sixty years have been spent here writing this book."[31] This would become *A Rebel's Vision Splendid*. He spent much of his time in the town of Grasmere, staying with a lifelong friend, May Davidson, in a district richly associated with writers and poets. From the window of her house he could see the old Swan Hotel, where, he wrote: "[Sir Walter] Scott used to go there when staying at Dove Cottage with [William] Wordsworth and [his sister] Dorothy."[32] On his second trip to Britain in 1927, Chapple began work on a third book, *The Turning Point of Truth*, which remains an unfinished manuscript. While there Chapple was offered ministerial charge of the church at Dundee in Scotland that Walter Walsh had once led. Unfortunately, he became unwell and could not accept the offer.[33]

Meanwhile, Unitarian services in Christchurch continued under the leadership of Rev. Clyde Carr and Norman Murray Bell, assisted by Fred Page and Lincoln Efford, both teachers in the Church's Socialist Sunday School. After Chapple returned to Christchurch in 1925 his ministry finished. He sold his house and moved to Tauranga. His decades of peace advocacy were recognised a few years after he retired, when William Lee Martin (1870-1950), MP for Raglan, nominated James Chapple for the Nobel Peace Prize in 1930. Lee Martin was Minister of Agriculture in the first Labour Government and later became a member of the Legislative Council. It was the third nomination of a New Zealander for a Nobel Prize and the first for peace. Although unsuccessful, it indicated the national standing of his work. That year the Nobel Peace Prize was awarded to a Swedish clergyman, Nathan Soderblom, for his efforts in promoting world peace.

The Christchurch church continued much as it had before James Chapple went on his travels until Clyde Carr joined the Labour Party. In 1928 he was elected Member of Parliament for the Timaru seat, which he held for the next 33 years. This left Norman Murray Bell in sole charge, which provided him with the opportunity to turn the church into the Free Religious Movement, which he did in late 1927.[34] A year later Clyde Carr reported that attendance at the Free Religious Movement was exceptionally good. He described Norman Murray Bell in very positive terms as "an undoubted scholar and a very likeable chap."[35]

Norman Murray Bell exerted his leadership in the new organisation when in 1932 he renamed the Socialist Sunday school the Socialist Guild of Youth, which met in the rooms of the No More War Movement in Chancery Lane. Children at the Guild school were taught freedom of thought and freedom of self-expression, and encouraged to be just and loving, and stand up for the weak and oppressed. Many who went through these schools became outspoken advocates for social justice and peace. In 1934 Norman Murray Bell's profile became more prominent when he launched *Cosmos: A Quarterly Journal of Pacifist Thought*, which was edited and printed at his own expense. Bell would provide copies free on request, though he did ask supporters for an annual subscription of two shillings. *Cosmos* included local and overseas information and published readers' letters. Its tone changed after 1939; from January 1940 it was headed "Wartime Series". Production devices also changed: copies were sometimes handwritten or hand typed rather than printed.

The next step occurred when Norman Murray Bell published his theological position for the Free Religious Movement in a 1935 issue of *Tomorrow*. Essentially summarised from his major theological work *A Gospel of Universal Compassion Being Another Side of Christianity*, it had an additional part stating the principles that "God is love" is a central dogma of religious belief, and that the application of agape (love that is wholly selfless and spiritual) applies to all individual and social problems. The principle of non-violent pacifism was advocated, and belief in vegetarianism and animal welfare work promoted.[36] What is not known is the extent to which regular attenders or members of the Free Religious Movement were in agreement with all or most of the principles laid out by Norman Murray Bell. The latter two principles, vegetarianism and animal welfare, were new and, as we will see, had been embraced by Norman Murray Bell just a few years before.

In the early years, between 1934 and 1938, more of the Movement's public lectures were delivered by guest speakers than by Norman Murray Bell.[37] One of the most controversial speakers was Professor Frederick Sinclaire, whose topics were "Devotion, the Bible and Religion" followed by "Not Spoiling our Old Faith". This must have come as a surprise to Norman Murray Bell.

Chapter 4

Sinclaire had completed an MA in English at Auckland University College, then received a scholarship to study for the ministry at Manchester College, Oxford. While at Manchester College, Sinclaire won the Dr Williams Theological Scholarship and was offered financial assistance to take an Oxford degree, which he did not take up. Instead, after completing his training he left for Australia, having taken a position at the Melbourne Unitarian Church at Eastern Hill. En route he married his New Zealand fiancée Esther Lewis (1873-1961) in Sydney, much to the surprise of his congregation on their arrival. His radical views led him into left-wing politics and peace movements. He was in conflict with the conservatives in the church, so he left to found the Free Religious Fellowship in 1911. In 1932 he returned to New Zealand to take up a chair in English Literature at Canterbury University College. While he seemed an ideal supporter of Norman Murray Bell's activities, he was now a congregant of the Anglican Church. His lectures to the Free Religious Movement in Christchurch, which urged a return to more traditional ecclesiastical practices, caused uproar amongst the Movement's adherents, which spilled into the local newspapers. Nevertheless, Bell and Sinclaire remained friends and continued to support each other in many political and social activities which they had in common.

In 1939 the Free Religious Movement's lectures were dominated by Norman Murray Bell, who delivered 22 lectures, mostly about pacifism. In 1940, however, only eight of the 19 lectures were by Norman Murray Bell; the other 11 were shared amongst other lecturers. Only a quarter had a pacifist theme. The remainder were of a general religious nature. At the 1941 annual Christmas party, while members enjoyed singing, games and competitions, and presentations were made to some hard-working members, a warm welcome was given to Norman Murray Bell, the "founder and chief lecturer of the movement."[38] The 1941 and 1942 lectures are an even greater mix: 32 lectures were advertised, of which Norman Murray Bell delivered 17. His old friend Professor Sinclaire gave an address on William Law (1686-1761), the influential Anglican priest who lost his position at Emmanuel College, Cambridge when he could not give his oath of allegiance to George I. In 1943 Norman Murray Bell gave 14 out of 33 lectures, and in 1944 he gave 27 out of 29.

By this time Norman Murray Bell's repertoire was less concerned with pacifism than with general religious topics and, in particular, comparative religions. The strong interest in the latter was stressed by the new leader of the Free Religious Movement, Will Hayes (1890-1959), who took over in 1931 following the death of Walter Walsh in London. Educated at a Quaker school and active in peace movements, Hayes was imprisoned during the Great War as a conscientious objector. Following a course of study at Manchester College, Oxford in 1927, he served his ministerial career at Chatham, Kent. There, as Brother John, he founded the Order of the Great Companions, which had as its main purpose encouraging the systematic study of world religions. He taught the precept of the brotherhood of humanity through the sisterhood of religions. A review after his death found that his contribution to the new discipline of Comparative Religion was unparalleled among dissenting scholars.[39]

Return to Academe

For a number of years before taking control of the Christchurch church and transforming it into the Free Religious Movement, Norman Murray Bell had been following his interest in comparative religion as an independent scholar. Having trained in classical studies and finding his interest piqued by the works of Walter Walsh, Bell explored Māori myths and religious beliefs. In 1928 he submitted a thesis on this subject to Canterbury University College for a Doctor of Literature.[40] He described religion as being defined by rites, which are actions performed by use of supernatural power to assure good; and myths, which he defined as the attribution to supernatural persons as explanations of events that cannot otherwise be explained. He wondered if it was possible to explain any of these factors in terms of contemporary human nature. He looked to the fundamental facts of human ontogeny — that is, human physiology and psychology — to provide a field where some of the roots of human rites and myths may be found. He decided to study the religious beliefs of Māori, as they were an important part of Polynesia; they were living in their original state until just over 100 years before his research began; there had been a long period of Māori isolation from foreign contact in Aotearoa; many

Māori rites and myths were well documented; there was a reliable oral tradition, and the Māori language was sufficiently well known to Europeans to allow researchers to undertake linguistic analysis. He aimed to find out if human ontogeny could provide a better understanding of how early Māori religion had developed. In carrying out his study he compared aspects of Māori myths with indigenous Australian and Abrahamic traditions. He made a detailed comparison of Māori creation myths, Rangi (Ranginui Father of sky or heaven) and Papa (Papatuanuku Mother of earth), with the Greek creation myth that all things are procreated by heaven and earth. He compared the belief that man is the son of earth and starry heaven in Māori mythology with the Hebrew myth of man being made out of dust. He looked at other ancient religions — Egyptian, Indian, and Phoenician — and at other Polynesian myths, from Tahiti and Hawaii. This approach of studying Māori mythology within comparative mythology on a worldwide scale was innovative for its time.

A thesis submitted to the College Registrar was required to embody the results of original work in a linguistic, literary, philosophical, or historical subject, which Bell's thesis did. However, the University of New Zealand list of doctoral theses (1912-1948) does not include the award of any degree to Norman Murray Bell. Under the University of New Zealand degree regulations for a Doctor of Literature, the thesis should be submitted to at least two teachers in the college nominated by the academic board, and unless a majority recommended to the contrary, it should then have been submitted to an examiner. There is no record of any examination of Norman Murray Bell's thesis. Of course, it is possible that the documents have been lost, and it is also possible that the initial assessors declined to recommend it proceed further. However, it is also possible that, due to the deprivation of civil rights imposed upon military defaulters for ten years from 10 December 1918, the view may have been taken that when Norman Murray Bell submitted his thesis, he was ineligible to be considered for a degree because of this legal penalty. The failure to have this work recognised must have been the cause of some chagrin as Norman Murray Bell later contemplated its publication and initially specified in his will that it ought to become publicly accessible, if it had not been published by the time of his death.[41]

Norman Murray Bell's involvement with Canterbury University College was renewed in 1936. First, the leave of absence of Dr H. D. Broadhead (1889-1967), lecturer in the Classics Department, created a temporary vacancy. (Dr Broadhead was an old friend and occasional speaker at the Free Religious Movement; both he and Norman Murray Bell had received scholarships to study classics at Trinity College, Cambridge). This resulted in the University Council appointing Norman Murray Bell to a relieving position to cover for Dr Broadhead for two terms. Secondly, Norman Murray Bell returned to undergraduate study, passing papers in Psychology I in 1936, Māori I and Hebrew I in 1938, Hebrew II in 1939, and Hebrew III in 1940. He also continued his interest in Māori anthropology with his membership of The Polynesian Society.

An Epiphany

Norman Murray Bell had been taking a great interest in psychology, both as a subject of study and in its application to individuals and society. He was a member of the Practical Psychology Club in Christchurch, where he lectured on "The Psychology of Dreams" in 1926, "Jung's Analytical Psychology" in 1927, and "The Psychology of Māori Tattooing" in 1934. However, his most interesting contribution to the Psychology Club was in October 1931, when he spoke on "Hallucination or Illumination: Psychology of Ecstatic Vision". This lecture was based on an experience he had on 5 December 1930, an event which he subsequently recorded.[42] Living at home with both his parents, the middle-aged Norman Murray Bell that December day had been following Gandhi's advice to keep his libido controlled by fasting, which he had now done for two days. He woke "with feelings of extraordinary wellbeing" which he found impossible to describe, though he believed it meant he was saved in a religious sense. He rushed to tell his father this good news and together they went to tell his mother. He next awoke in his mother's bed; she was stroking his forehead and the family doctor was present. (Some time must have elapsed for the doctor to be called to the house.) The doctor informed Bell that he had had four paroxysms and had struggled with his mother, striking her on the nose. He recorded that in his mental state he "seemed to see the whole of creation rolled up, what had been evolved or unrolled was now being rolled up again … as the rolling up took place, I looked on to see what was happening... I saw how everything fitted exactly into the universal scheme of things." This experience "was to show me God (I was to see 'Love' face to face — did I identify God & Love actually in the vision? I feel somewhat doubtful in this now tho' it fits in). What I actually saw was my mother's face."

In his vision Norman Murray Bell "saw how the whole scheme of evolution was just & good in its very essence." He also saw his mother again and told her that she had had a hard time, but that he loved her, and he reassured her everything would be all right. It was, he wrote, something he knew, but it was impossible to describe "... this 'known' — my whole being, not my mere intellect..." He went on to think he may have compared himself to the message Paul gave about a man "being caught up into the seventh [sic, should be third] heaven and saw things not lawful to utter" (Corinthians 2:12). He then felt he must get back to earth, and during this time he struggled violently with his parents who were trying to hold him down. Notwithstanding St. Paul's injunction, Norman Murray Bell revealed what he saw was the key to salvation: the protection of the whole of creation without exception: plants, animals and humans. "I had grasped the whole scheme of creation from top to bottom... there is no doubt about this being genuine."

Norman Murray Bell's experience was not unique; many instances are to be found within a range of religious and philosophical traditions. Significantly, he included "ecstatic" in the title of his talk, which has within its meaning: of the nature of a trance, catalepsy, mystical absorption, stupor or frenzy, amongst the experiences to which a person may be subject.[43] However, he did not attempt to place his own experiences within the broader historical or psychological knowledge of these experiences.

The classic work on the subject remains *The Varieties of Religious Experience* by William James, first published in 1902.[44] Bell experienced many of the features that James discusses as typical of the mystical state, especially the sense of being at one with the universe or its creator, gaining universal insight or revelation, and the authority derived from the mystical state. For example, the experience of John Trevor, founder of the Labour Church movement in Britain, has similar features to that of Norman Murray Bell. Trevor's experience occurred in the Cheshire

Hills in the late nineteenth century: "The consciousness of the eternal oneness of things sank deep into my heart," he wrote in his autobiography. He wrote that his "experiences…of God's presence have been rare and brief" but that when they occurred he became "aware that I was immersed in the infinite ocean of God." He also wrote, "There is yourself, the universe, God. Live faithfully by what you are…The gifts of God cannot be communicated or transferred."[45]

Even humanists and sceptics are not immune from such mystical experiences, as Bertrand Russell reported. In 1901 Russell found himself in another realm of thought, reflecting on the unendurable loneliness of the human soul which can only be reached by the sort of love religious teachers have preached. After this experience he became a completely different person: "For a time a sort of mystic illumination possessed me." He had a profound desire to find a philosophy that would make human life endurable and became a lifelong committed pacifist.[46] More recent research into what are described as self-transcendent experiences supports the view that mystical events (feelings of awe, rapture or time stopping together with a sense of unity with other people, nature, God or the universe), are relatively common and occur amongst many cultures. Now neuroscience and psychophysiology are providing insights into the involvement of brain regions and physiological processes in such events, which may lead to more profound understanding.[47]

For Norman Murray Bell this ecstatic experience was a life-changing event, which caused him to embrace vegetarianism and animal welfare with the same ardour he pursued peace. He joined the Humanitarian and Anti-Vivisection Society of New Zealand, becoming Christchurch branch President in 1935. In 1936 the Society moved into the rooms in Chancery Lane which also served as the meeting place for the peace organisations and Free Religious Movement that Norman Murray Bell headed. Abandoned animals were rescued and campaigns were undertaken as Norman Murray Bell sought to get the message of animal rights and vegetarianism out to the public via letters to newspapers, articles in magazines, leaflet distribution, public meetings and radio talks.[48]

5

The Second World War and Its Aftermath, 1940-1962

Pacifism During World War II

1940 was a portentous year for New Zealand, marking the centenary of British colonisation in New Zealand. The government began its centennial planning well before 1940, opening the Centennial Exhibition on 8 November 1939, two months after the outbreak of World War II. The Exhibition spread over 55 acres in Wellington and ran for six months, portraying the national spirit of New Zealand as its dominating theme. The Exhibition was one element of what was to be a year of celebrations. Local pageants were held throughout the country. Christchurch began its celebration with a long procession of floats and hundreds of people in pioneer dress. The Canterbury Centennial Music Festival was held at the Theatre Royal, Christchurch. (These celebrations were not as grand as they might have been; Canterbury wanted to have its own centennial celebrations just a decade later, which was to be the showpiece for the province.) Meanwhile, another and more important centennial event was held on the southern coast of Banks Peninsula at Akaroa. There 500 Māori gathered, the largest assembly ever in the South Island, to welcome guests at an official ceremony. The official party, some 200 strong, was led by the Governor-General, Lord Galway, and included the Prime Minister and many cabinet ministers. Courteously greeting the officials, the Māori speakers expressed the hope that the Prime Minister would respond to their land claims. They reminded their guests of this outstanding grievance when speaking about the British assertion of sovereignty over the South Island. However, the politicians would not deal with the issue and swept it aside, much to the dismay of the attending Māori.

Music was prominent in the festival planning. In the National Centennial Competition for original compositions Douglas Lilburn achieved notable success. He received first and second prizes for orchestral works *Drysdale Overture* and *Festival Overture* and first prize for his choral work *Prodigal Country*. The works of Lilburn were premiered in a nationwide radio broadcast on 23 November 1940 as the opening pieces in a concert of New Zealand music.[1] Lilburn had returned early that year after three years of study at the Royal College of Music in London. While there he had been part of a small group of expatriate New Zealanders "united in their leftist leanings ... and revulsion to war (as distinct from pacifism) ..."[2] Now he re-established connections with the artistic friends he had known in 1937 and even moved back into his old Christchurch flat in Cambridge Terrace. Douglas Lilburn developed a relationship with the artist Rita Angus, a committed pacifist. Later he introduced her to the orchestral and choral work "Dona Nobis Pacem"

Douglas Lilburn conducting the National Symphony Orchestra, 1948

Chapter 5

by the English composer Ralph Vaughan Williams. (The title of the work, which means "Give us Peace", is a phrase in the Agnus Dei section of the Catholic Mass. Vaughan Williams was a pacifist and had been Lilburn's tutor in composition at the Royal College of Music). This led to Rita's painting of the same name, her largest work; it comprised a portrait of Vaughan Williams surrounded by symbols of peace, images of fertility and New Zealand motifs. By then it appears Lilburn had a deeper sympathy toward pacifism.[3]

The Christchurch City Council took the opportunity in 1940 to invite public proposals for a new city motto. The original motto, "Britons Hold Your Own", was a direct reflection of the settlers' origins; for some this was good enough while others advocated for change. Included in the 38 suggestions that came forth was one from Norman Murray Bell. His suggestion was unique, in that it was not derived from the Bible, Latin or English maxims: he proposed a Māori saying "poua te tatau pounamu", which he translated as: "close the greenstone door", meaning "make a lasting peace". Needless to say, this far-sighted epitome of bi-cultural recognition was not chosen by the city fathers.[4] Instead, they opted for a complex Latin motto that reflected English ecclesiastical origins, the fulfilment of the founders' faith and bold claims for Canterbury's future, with no consideration for the inhabitants who had preceded the Canterbury Pilgrims and now lived alongside them. Norman Murray Bell's proposal was the only one which was inclusive and showed consideration for Māori. He was probably uniquely placed amongst his contemporaries in his attitude towards Māori: recognising the wrongs inflicted by colonisation on them, studying Māori religion and culture and recognising the importance of Parihaka in New Zealand's peace history.

Pacifism had shallow roots in the general population, and it was not long before public derision turned to hostility, as patriotism conflated pacifism with communism and sedition. University students were often targeted, as the pacifist minority were well known for publicly expressing unpopular views; somewhat surprisingly they were also punished by the university authorities.[5] For the wider pacifist community, however, it was one thing to be subject to public hostility and contempt during peacetime but quite another during wartime. The government led a determined policy to suppress the expression of any opinion opposed to the war, including opposition on any grounds to the official war policy of the day. These actions had a chilling effect on the expression of anti-war convictions for many individuals who were silenced because of fear of public reprisal or official sanction. For others in the peace movement the brutal aggression waged by the fascist nations led to a reconsideration of their beliefs, and the decision, however reluctantly, to support the war. Those of military age who did not succumb to this pressure were at legal jeopardy, and upon conviction faced either defaulters' detention camp or prison. Thus the peace movement became seriously weakened as the war progressed.

Leaders of the anti-war movements, many of whom had experience of social and official repression during the Great War, had anticipated such a reaction. In October 1939 the leaders of the main pacifist organisations in Christchurch came together and formed a Combined Pacifist Committee. Archibald Barrington pronounced Christchurch "a hotbed of pacifists of all kinds working together,"[6] an apt description for the committee comprising Charles Mackie from the Peace Council, the Quaker John Johnson, Norman Murray Bell from the No More War Movement, Thurlow Thompson from the Peace Pledge Union, and Lincoln Efford, who worked tirelessly for the last two organisations. Their immediate aim was to ensure the city council would continue to allow pacifists to hold public meetings. In this they succeeded; unlike other cities, Christchurch, which had a long free speech tradition, allowed meetings into 1940.[7] Following a meeting the Combined Pacifist Committee held with a permit, the police had to escort the speakers from the park when the crowd, largely comprised of soldiers, pushed one of them from the platform. The City Council held a hearing into the event, attended by members of the pacifist committee including Thurlow Thompson, Lincoln Efford, Frederick Sinclaire, and Norman Murray Bell, who argued they had not caused the trouble and had faithfully complied with the terms of their permit. These facts were not disputed. However, the Returned Soldiers Association, which was present, argued that the pacifists should be suppressed because their beliefs were in conflict with the government's recruiting campaign. The City Council agreed and voted by ten votes to four not to allow pacifist

Chapter 5

street meetings.[8] Thus the last effective public peace campaigning in New Zealand was suppressed. Or was it?

Just as important for the cause was the establishment of the co-operative pacifist press in a room adjoining Chancery Lane, managed and operated by Lincoln Efford. The Co-operative Press was instrumental in producing most of the country's anti-war literature during the nine months it operated, including the pamphlets *What Are We Fighting For?*, *The Road to Peace*, *The Economic Causes of War* and *A Pacifist Peace Settlement (preliminary draft)*. In June 1940 the printing press of the Co-operative Press was seized by the police under the Public Safety Emergency Regulations (effective from 21 February 1940). None of its publications had been found subversive by a Court, but no such decision was required; mere suspicion was sufficient. This was just the beginning, as the publisher of the current affairs magazine *Tomorrow* was to find out: this publication was effectively suppressed as no printer would take the risk of losing their press to the police. Under a broadened definition of what was subversive, the Emergency Regulations gave the police power to prohibit meetings, arrest speakers and search without warrant. Additional powers were extended under the Censorship and Publicity Regulations on 29 May 1940, strengthening the seizure of printing presses which produced subversive material, including material detrimental to the war effort. (The regulation was drawn so broadly that a typewriter could be included in the term "printing press".) Editors of newspapers were given direction on what could and could not be published and personal letters were opened and examined by the censors. Both Norman Murray Bell and Lincoln Efford were subject to frequent home searches by police exercising these powers without warrants.

Once freedom of speech was dealt with, a raft of further restrictions on human rights was introduced. The National Service Emergency Regulations of June 1940 provided for conscription of men aged 18 to 46, although no soldier under 21 was to serve overseas. Under these Regulations, a reserve force for home defence was created. (Both men and women in civilian life could be directed to work in essential war industries.) An Anti-Conscription Council was formed led by Norman Murray Bell, Lincoln Efford, James Saunders and Dr Robert

The Second World War and Its Aftermath

Lincoln Efford

Roy Douglas Milligan (1893-1963). The latter had served in the New Zealand Army medical corps in World War I. He was a medical practitioner who founded the Christchurch branch of the League of Nations Union, and went to Geneva in 1936 as an observer at the League on behalf of the New Zealand Government. In May 1940 the Council obtained support from trade unions for their opposition to conscription but were unable to seek a public platform because of the Emergency Regulations.

To help men resisting conscription, a Fellowship of Conscientious Objectors was formed in 1941 with Lincoln Efford as secretary. (For Norman Murray Bell it was a feeling of *déjà vu*, as twenty years earlier he had formed an organisation with the same name to work for the release of conscientious objectors held after the war ended. Now he was helping Lincoln Efford, who shouldered much of the work.) Efford attended appeal board meetings and helped men prepare their submissions. One magistrate accused Efford of helping the enemy and charged him with contempt. Efford suggested he be charged with treason instead and the matter was dropped.

Chapter 5

There were 3,077 appeals, of which only 20 per cent were allowed, and these men were directed to do specified civil work. Of the remainder, 40 per cent were sent to non-combatant service and 40 per cent of appeals were dismissed.[9] Over 800 men were sentenced to defaulters' camps, some after first serving a few months in prison. They automatically lost the right to vote and, if they were teachers, they lost their positions for the duration of the war. Under the Teachers (Conscientious Objectors and Defaulters) Regulations 1941, the mere fact of exercising an appeal against conscription on the ground of conscientious objection automatically resulted in dismissal.

An unforeseen event would provide the opportunity for the anti-war lobby to largely circumvent the prohibition on public communication of their message. Following the death of Tim Armstrong (1875-1942), Member of Parliament for Christchurch East, a by-election was held in February 1943. This created the opportunity for the pacifist movement to present their message to the general public without being censored or suppressed by the authorities. Lincoln Efford stood as a peace candidate supported by a campaign committee of well-known leaders of the peace movement, including Norman Murray Bell; Basil Cairns Dowling (1910-2000), one of the Bloomsbury South group whose poetry was published by the Caxton Press; and Colin Marshall Curtis (1919-2002), an exempted conscientious objector and humanitarian socialist. (Dowling, who held an MA from Canterbury University College, was disillusioned with the church and had abandoned his studies for the Presbyterian ministry.) Together these three produced and distributed 30,000 election leaflets. Other pacifist leaders who chaired or spoke at Efford's meetings included: Charles Mackie, John Johnson, Dr Robert Roy Douglas Milligan, Thurlow Thompson and Anglican Archdeacon Frederick Norman Taylor (1871-1960), MA (Oxon.) who became a prominent clergyman following his arrival in New Zealand in 1913. Frederick Taylor had three sons, all of whom followed their father as priests in the Anglican Church: David Mortimer Taylor (1910-1995) and Roger Patrick Taylor (1912-1993), both born in England, and John Humphrey Taylor (1919-2007), born New Zealand. Father and sons were devoted advocates of pacifism both within the church and in the public arena.

During the by-election campaign the current Prime Minister, Peter Fraser (1884-1950) described Efford as a man with a foolish utopian idea. Yet Fraser's condemnation of the dream of peace during wartime appeared incongruous, if not hypocritical, since he himself had opposed conscription during World War I, and served twelve months in prison for sedition. The election was comfortably won by Mabel Howard (1894-1972) for the Labour Party, followed by the National Party candidate, with Lincoln Efford a distant third with only 114 votes — a serious setback for organised pacifism. Efford thought this reflected, in part, denial of radio access and restricted press coverage.

Before the war the Christian Pacifist Society had been well supported by the Methodist Church, with about a third of all its ministers being members at the outbreak of war, but in May 1940 the Methodist Church's "Manifesto on Peace and War," which banned either recruitment or resistance to military service from the pulpit, was endorsed by Annual Conference.[10] This dealt a severe blow to the Christian Pacifist Society. Ormond Burton, unable to reconcile his conscience to the discipline of the church, was forced to give up his ministry when the church dismissed him in 1942. (Burton was not reunited with the church until 1955.) The other main support before the war came from the Presbyterian Church; but shortly after the outbreak of war it too decided in principle to support the war. The four main Presbyteries agreed on a position which was endorsed by the General Assembly of the Presbyterian Church in November 1939. It stated that the war was just and urged its members to realise their civic responsibility in accepting service when required by the authorities; some church members might bear arms, some would refuse and adopting either course could express loyalty to the will of God. Connie Jones (1919-2008), a young Methodist who had attended the Socialist Guild of Youth run by Norman Murray Bell, had joined the Christian Pacifist Society in 1937 when it had about 300 members. In 1941 she was sentenced to three months in prison, the only woman to be imprisoned for pacifist activity in World War II. After her release she married John Summers (1916-1993), a Quaker who served in the New Zealand Army Medical Corps during the war. By the time of the 1943 elections the Christian Pacifist Society, which had been one of the strongest peace groups, was reduced to holding house meetings amongst the remnant of its membership.

Chapter 5

The general election in September 1943 allowed the pacifists to engage with the public on a large scale. Four candidates stood on the peace platform. There were three members from the Christian Pacifist Society: Ronald Charles Howell (1912-1985) standing in Auckland East electorate; Archibald Barrington (1906-1986) in Wellington East; and Arthur Herbert Carman (1902-1982) in Wellington North. Lincoln Efford stood in Christchurch South. Lincoln Efford saw the election as an opportunity for the various peace organisations to come together in an organised national campaign, but this did not eventuate. All four seats were held by members of the government. There was no coordination amongst the peace candidates; they each ran their own campaign. With about 80 per cent of households having a radio in 1940, being kept off the air was a major setback for the minor party candidates. The government censor ruled that the peace candidates should not criticise government war policy. Nor were they allowed to promote independence for India, which was held to be seditious. The outcome was a foregone conclusion: the Labour government was returned to office with a comfortable majority of ten seats over its conservative rival the National Party, and only one Independent was elected. The campaign was not a wasted effort, however. The four peace candidates collectively polled about 1,000 votes and put out a message favouring peace by negotiation, fairer treatment of conscientious objectors and better conditions for those incarcerated for their beliefs.

The month following the general election Charles Mackie died. This was a further blow to the already weakened peace movement. With the veteran leader of the National Peace Council gone the organisation might have fallen with him. Lincoln Efford stepped up and in addition to his other activities became the National Peace Council secretary. As the war continued so did the activities of the Fellowship of Conscientious Objectors, with branches in Auckland, Wellington, Christchurch and Dunedin. The Fellowship fought until the last inmate was released from defaulters' camp in 1946. For the remaining core of peace advocates, the teaching that "Faith is the substance of things hoped for, the evidence of things not seen" (Hebrews 11:1) appears appropriate.

The war had taken its toll on Frederick Sinclaire, who became very disheartened by the outbreak of hostilities. Already unwell, his health deteriorated further, and he suffered increasingly from bouts of depression. The once forceful peace advocate became a shadow of his former self. His friend and biographer H. Winston Rhodes wrote: "Other indications of his mental and bodily distress were, unfortunately, becoming only too apparent to me, for we were in daily communication in our rooms at the University."[11] He became unable to carry out the role of Head of the English Department and Winston Rhodes unobtrusively took over its administration. Frederick Sinclaire retired in 1948.

Norman Murray Bell continued to produce his publication *Cosmos: A Journal of Pacifist Thought*. With the closure of the Co-operative Press, however, he lost his printer. Not one to be discouraged, he began producing *Cosmos* at home on a duplicator. When his duplicator was seized in a police raid and *Cosmos* declared to be a seditious publication, he began producing a handwritten version. To evade detection and seizure, Norman Murray Bell walked the streets of Christchurch, often at night, delivering his magazine and occasional leaflets. He had already been pilloried by the conservative politician Carey John Carrington (1877-1966), a member of the Upper House of Parliament, the Legislative Council, who demanded that *Cosmos* be suppressed and Norman Murray Bell jailed for his disloyalty. Bell had other confrontations with officialdom: earlier in the war he decided he could not in all conscience support the military through his tax payments. He deducted the amount he thought was compromised from his annual tax return and suggested it be paid to the then "Native" [Māori] Department to acknowledge the wrongs done to Māori by the Imperial and colonial military. He was threatened with prosecution by the Commissioner of Taxes unless he paid in full, but no action was taken. Later in the war, he refused to enrol in the Emergency Reserve Corps which would have directed him into work in support of the war effort, and once again was not prosecuted.[12] Perhaps wiser heads than Mr Carrington's prevailed, recognising how dangerous it might be to make a martyr out of this now ageing peace activist. These stands taken by Norman Murray Bell echo the case made by Henry David Thoreau (1817-1862), who argued in his famous essay *Civil Disobedience* for following one's conscience and not blindly accepting government policy.

Chapter 5

Ethical and Religious Thought: Idealism and Social Justice

By the end of the war, Norman Murray Bell's theological position had evolved considerably. At the time he studied divinity at London University and wrote *A Gospel of Universal Compassion Being Another Side of Christianity*, his approach to theological matters was not only orthodox but appeared quite traditional. A decade later, when he established the Free Religious Movement in Christchurch, his outlook was less orthodox, although it must be remembered that the Free Religious Movement held itself to be:

> ... essentially religious; but it is not a sect or a church; for it operates in all sects and churches, yet outside and independently of them all. It substitutes the humanist for the dogmatic, ethics for creeds, and the collective service of [hu]mankind for sacraments. It regards religion as spiritual enthusiasm directing itself towards reform of abuses, just social order, free economic conditions, and pacific international arrangements.[13]

In addition to being a step away from his earlier orthodoxy, the Free Religious Movement had a framework that encouraged open inquiry into religious beliefs. This outlook allowed for the ongoing development of Norman Murray Bell's views. By December of 1944, when discussing the correct Greek translation of "peace on earth, goodwill towards men" (Luke 2:14), he commented: "From a social point of view the word 'God' may symbolise for us the unity reasonably (perhaps) presumed to exist through the multiplicity of our universe."[14]

We can see affinities in this description with the thoughts of some twentieth-century theologians, such as Dietrich Bonhoeffer (1906-1945). Bonhoeffer took a unique approach in his 1930 doctoral thesis, *The Communion of Saints*, combining sociological and theological disciplines in understanding the church; and in his 1931 second doctoral thesis, *Act and Being*, which dealt with the influence of transcendental philosophy derived from Kantian idealism. Bonhoeffer spent a year studying at the Union Theological Seminary in New York, where he was exposed to American racism, which greatly affected him and helped shape his views on German antisemitism. His work during the war on Christian ethics, published after his death in a Nazi prison, opposed the separation of the sacred and the profane and the dualism of the church in the world, replacing it with one unified ethic based on the person and work of Christ. This, he believed, would remove the sense of otherworldliness and free Christianity for its work in this world. The other modern theologian Norman Murray Bell shows some affinity with is Paul Tillich (1886-1965). Tillich's opposition to the Nazis led to him being barred from German universities and he took up a position at Union Theological Seminary in New York. He was critical of the anthropomorphic God relatively widespread in Christianity; instead, he understood God as part of the structure of all living things and the "ground of Being-Itself."[15] He appreciated the use of symbols to envision something as abstract as God. Tillich was also interested in the human condition, applying the findings of psychoanalysis and existentialist philosophy when discussing this problem.

Norman Murray Bell devoted his life to living his ideals and beliefs. His religious-ethical beliefs were expressed in political action, which was broadly compatible with the social gospel movement. This movement grew out of the late nineteenth-century reaction to unbridled capitalism. Achieving strong inter-denominational acceptance, it spread throughout developed western nations, applying Christian social ethics to a multitude of social problems. For many in New Zealand, the newly formed Labour Party was a political version of applied Christian social ethics, so it is unsurprising that it formed the framework for Norman Murray Bell's world view. Following his release from prison after World War I, he became active in the Labour Party. The principles of social democracy — the building of a just society whereby there would be a peaceful transition from capitalism to socialism within the established constitutional process — appealed to his moral sense. Norman Murray Bell lived in a time of violent revolution in parts of Europe, when some saw revolution as the only hope for change. Bell realised that participating in a democracy that allowed economic reform in the interest of all the people was a *sine qua non*. He had an important insight that for participatory democracy to be fulfilled in society, citizens must be well educated and given every opportunity to engage in robust public debate. He was one of the first to understand the importance of popular communication through the radio. From the earliest days of its introduction, he campaigned to ensure access to promote the messages of peace, international cooperation, social justice, animal welfare and public education and debate.

As the great depression continued to ravage the world economies, the New Zealand Labour Party was elected to power for the first time in 1935. The new Labour government offered economic and social security: it nationalised sections of the economy such as banking, mining, and broadcasting and implemented public works, state house building on a large scale and a guaranteed price scheme for dairy products to assist farmers. The welfare state was expanded under the Social Security Act of 1938; its major provisions included free health services, extended pension schemes for the elderly, welfare cover for the sick and unemployment benefits for those out of work. All these policies promoted the ideals Norman Murray Bell fought for, and must have allowed him to express his religious and ethical beliefs in this particular political form. Similarly, we can conclude that his awareness of the inequalities and suffering caused by the unreformed capitalist system, an absence of social democracy and inadequate provision of social welfare, shaped his views of society and led him to support political labour and trade union movements.

Norman Murray Bell's main preoccupation was the ethics of pacifism: peace advocacy, the conduct of the war at home and abroad, and preparations for life after the war. He expressed his ethical positions at meetings of the Free Religious Movement, which welcomed these views; in his *Cosmos* magazine; and in his voluminous newspaper correspondence. He continued to argue publicly that "maiming and killing women and children and of civilians, whether by British or German, American or Japanese airman is an offence against God and man."[16] Norman Murray Bell identified the main cause of World War II, finding it in the Treaty of Versailles signed after the Great War which imposed crushing reparations on Germany. These economic factors would remain important considerations when he discussed what should happen after the present war. He wrote:

> It is for Christians, first, to stress the ideal of fraternity to be realised economically through economic equality; second, to emphasise the paradox that freedom is realised by man through devotion to what is ideal and not through domination, whether economic, political, or ideological.[17]

Bell wanted more public discussion on war aims and plans for the peace. He knew it was important to plan for more than just victory. There were many countries where the establishment of democratic principles was needed to ensure political freedom. In particular, he was concerned about the incompatibility of democracy with the notion of the empire. He liked to point out that the British Empire was ruled by a mere 70 million whites. "We ought by our own principle", he wrote, "be giving back self-government to 420 [million] coloured men and women."[18] This reinforced a position he had long advocated of independence for Samoa and India. He placed great store on the principles contained within the Atlantic Charter, devised by Britain and the United States: an end to territorial ambitions; changes to territories based on the wishes of the people affected; the right to self-determination for all people; open market access for all countries on equal terms; global economic co-operation and improved social welfare; freedom of the seas; and disarmament of the axis powers followed by universal disarmament after the war.

The Charter was widely adopted amongst the allied countries and on 1 January 1942, a larger group of Charter nations signed the "Declaration by United Nations," which became the basis for the United Nations organisation. For Norman Murray Bell, the Charter and Declaration embodied many of the principles he thought ought to govern world affairs. He singled out clause three, right to self-determination for all people, and clause four, reduction of trade barriers and open market access, as being "most useful for human progress towards world unity." He went on to say: "The main difficulty is that the authors of the Charter do not practice them."[19] Like many who had lived through the period that exposed the weakness and failures of the League of Nations, he was determined to see that politicians did far more to ensure that the new world system would be given every chance of success.

Animal rights and welfare were never far from Norman Murray Bell's public advocacy. He attacked the "thoughtless cruelty of man's treatment to his weaker kinsmen" during the duck shooting season, which he attributed to a "primitive blood-lust with no thought for the inalienable rights of fellow living beings."[20] On the feast day of St Francis of Assisi, patron saint of animals and the environment, he wrote: "Long before the days of scientific biology this saint had grasped the unity and universal kinship of terrestrial life." And he argued that humans should treat "the less-developed as you would like the more-developed to treat you: that is the golden rule in its evolutionary form."[21] Many pacifists, being ethically opposed to all killing, were also vegetarians, and both were natural allies in the advocacy of animal welfare. Vegetarian societies realised that economic necessity could lead to meat-eating and vegetarianism could only "flourish where there was enough income to afford an abundance of food."[22] This point was not lost on Norman Murray Bell, who saw economic equality as an integral part of the struggle for social justice. His strong pacifism and animal ethics were imbued with the Schweitzerian principle of reverence for life.

As president of the Free Religious Movement, Norman Murray Bell wrote to the Prime Minister urging the abolition of the death penalty and seeking the commuting of a prisoner's death sentence.[23] He called on the Prime Minister to investigate the state of mental hospitals, to provide scientific treatment by qualified psychologists and establish halfway houses and convalescent houses for patients.[24]

These positions were in step with New Zealand's first penal reform society, formed in Canterbury by the poet Blanche Edith Baughan (1870-1958). After her education at Royal Holloway College, London University, where she achieved a BA in Classics, Blanche Baughan was a social worker in the east end slums of London. Settling in Christchurch in 1902, she was a contemporary and friend of the feminist poet Jessie Mackay (1864-1938) and Ursula Bethell, moving in the same circle as Bloomsbury South. One summer morning in 1905 Blanche Baughan had an intense transcendent experience, which she described as:

> I had no sense of time or place. The ecstasy was terrific while it lasted. It can only have lasted a minute or two. It went as suddenly as it came. I found myself bathed with tears, but they were tears of joy. I felt ONE with everything and everybody: and somehow I knew that what I had experienced was Reality, and that Reality was Perfection.[25]

This experience took her beyond her early years of Anglicanism and into mysticism. She had an affinity with the writings of the American Transcendentalists and the poetry of Walt Whitman. She also took a keen interest in social reform, including animal welfare and the welfare

The Second World War and Its Aftermath

Blanche Edith Baughan

of the sick and handicapped, especially those with mental handicaps. She was a volunteer nurse during the 1918 influenza epidemic, and a strong advocate for the abolition of capital punishment. Motivated by her intense spiritual experience, Blanche Baughan's main mission in life became the more humane treatment of prisoners. In 1924 she formed the Howard League for Prison Reform based on the British model of the same name, which opposed flogging and capital punishment (in New Zealand both were abolished in 1941), advocating prisoner rehabilitation, education, and psychological assessments. She was supported by other members of the peace movement including Charles Mackie, Lincoln Efford (who became secretary and president of the League), and Ormond Burton. Norman Murray Bell joined her in providing concerts and lectures to prison inmates. There was also wide support within the Free Religious Movement, and Connie Summers (née Jones) held open discussions on prison reform at the Movement's rooms in Chancery Lane.[26]

Chapter 5

The Struggle for Peace Continues, 1946-1962

By the time the war formally ended on 2 September 1945, the world was no longer the same place it had been on 1 September 1939: about 85 million people had died, or 3 per cent of the world population, making it the deadliest conflict in history. The systematic genocide carried out in concentration camps had murdered about six million mostly Jewish people. Two atomic bombs had been dropped on Japan in August 1945 ushering in the era of weapons of mass destruction. Virtually everything the peace cause had fought for had been lost. For those who were not faint hearted, the struggle for world peace and social justice was about to begin again.

The most important event in the New Zealand peace calendar after the war was the National Peace Conference in Christchurch in June 1946, organised by Lincoln Efford. The conference attracted over a hundred attendees to some of its most sought-after sessions. Confer-

Norman Murray Bell outside his house at 134 Geraldine Street, c.1950

The Second World War and Its Aftermath

Norman Murray Bell and a friend on a cycling trip, 1950s

ence proposals included international disarmament, the establishment of a Ministry of Peace, and the removal of radio censorship. The latter topic was one dear to Norman Murray Bell's heart and he is likely to have proposed it. (Unfortunately there appear to be no records of the Conference that would determine this.) Efford proposed a New Zealand Pacifist Council as a common organisation to which all pacifist entities could amalgamate. This proposal failed to gain support. One who resisted it completely was Norman Murray Bell, who declared that he wanted to retain the No More War Movement identity, arguing that a number of separate organisations could achieve more than one large one. The failure to bring about significant amalgamation amongst the peace movement was underscored by the minor union of the Peace Council and the Peace Pledge Union into the Peace Union, though even this would fail by 1952. The various peace organisations were tired, run down and barely functioning.

Chapter 5

The No More War Movement was supported by a handful of Norman Murray Bell's friends. He was living in the family home with his sister Winifred Doris; they were alone following the death of their father Horace, who died in September 1945, ten years after his wife. In 1947 the Movement lobbied to have controversial radio topics given air time and gained Labour Party support for this. In 1949 the Movement organised a petition to abolish compulsory military training. This was the last time it was active, then it too shut down. However, the issue of compulsory national service in peacetime only arose because of the cold war and the opposition fought back under the banner of the Peace and Anti-Conscription Federation. In the resulting 1949 public referendum, the Labour government received approval for conscription but was then voted out of office. In July that year, the University of Cambridge conferred an MA degree on Norman Murray Bell, in absentia, under the regulation which permits a BA graduate to receive an MA degree not less than six years after beginning their first degree.

Now confronting the atomic arms issue, the Peace Union under Lincoln Efford's leadership organised the first Hiroshima Day march in 1947 in Christchurch. The anti-nuclear weapons campaign was boosted with the public opposition to nuclear testing, particularly in the Pacific. In 1957 two petitions were organised opposing nuclear weapons testing in any territory and calling on the three nuclear powers, the United States, Great Britain and the Soviet Union, to stop making or using nuclear weapons. One petition was organised by the Quakers, the other by Norman Murray Bell, who was campaigning without any organisational backing. His petition also pointed out that these weapons posed "a threat to the well-being not only of mankind but of all life on this earth."[27] While Norman Murray Bell was working alone he attracted support from Elsie Locke (1912-2001), who would go on to become the doyenne of the peace movement in New Zealand.[28] She organised a roster of volunteers and helped collect signatures for his petition, describing her experience as follows:

> Norman Murray Bell had grown old and the No More War Movement had faded away, but his patience and persistence had endured. Deeply upset by the H-bomb escalations and free of any political allegiances, I was among those who offered to help with his petition tables in

Hiroshima Day march, August 6, 1961
Left: Rev. Alan Brash. Right: Lincoln Efford

Cathedral Square, Christchurch. People unused to petitions went scurrying past, as if afraid to discover what it was all about: we had to call out and tell them. Under the apparent indifference we found many worried people. Norman Bell followed this up with cards to be signed and sent to the Prime Minister.[29]

Elsie Locke noted the effect of helping Norman Murray Bell meant for her: "This modest activity was the beginning of my own long involvement with the anti-nuclear movement."[30] Her impressions of Norman Murray Bell were that he was not a crank and was highly educated and widely read. He would not use any product which involved the slaughter or exploitation of animals: his shoes were made from a sort of plastic and he did not touch food containing milk or eggs.[31]

When the two petitions were presented to Parliament in October 1957, both were given the high recommendation of "most favourable consideration". They were referred to the Government and there they languished. By now it may have dawned on Norman Murray Bell that the age in which he achieved so much and expected to achieve more

Chapter 5

had faded away; now it was beyond his grasp. However, his activities in conjunction with the members of the movements he led, together with friends and colleagues in kindred organisations, set the stage for what was to follow: the great struggle for the survival of humanity in the atomic age.

It would be an inauspicious year for the peace movement, animal welfare, vegetarianism and social justice causes generally when in 1962 two towering figures died within months of each other. Lincoln Efford, who had not enjoyed good health since inadequate medical care following a rugby injury in 1927, died, aged 54, on 24 April 1962. Then three months later Norman Murray Bell died, aged 75, on 5 August 1962.

Going Forward: Prophecy Fulfilled and a Voice Un-stilled

Norman Murray Bell can rightly be regarded as a prophet in his time. He evinced the prophetic spirit discussed by Allen Curnow: in times when a terrible calamity is foreseen, such as war, the authentic voice of prophecy springs from the compulsion to address the nation and provide a warning to all of humanity. Although Norman Murray Bell's lifelong devotion to the cause of peace could not avert World War II, he continued the struggle when peace returned. In planning and undertaking his activities he showed independence born of his intellectual temperament; in this regard he did not fit closely into the broader peace movement, preferring to lead rather than follow.

Because of the limitations on source material what we have mainly seen is the public man, his ideas and actions, but very little of the private person. Despite these constraints, we know enough about Norman Murray Bell's beliefs to imagine how he would have responded to later developments. In the decades following his death, many of Norman Murray Bell's aspirations were realised or brought closer. These are events he would have embraced with a sense of fulfilment. He would also have been saddened by other events that detracted from his ideals.

Bell would certainly have welcomed the New Zealand government's opposition to French nuclear testing in the Pacific. This culminated in New Zealand taking a case to the International Court of Justice in The Hague in 1974, resulting in France stopping atmospheric testing.

(France struck back ten years later, in 1985, sending secret agents to sink the Greenpeace ship, the *Rainbow Warrior*, which was moored in Auckland, New Zealand, ready to lead a protest at continued French underground testing in the Pacific. Two of the agents were captured and convicted, leading to a political confrontation between New Zealand and France, which was resolved by the United Nations.) For Norman Murray Bell the presence of a United Nations organisation and institutions upholding rule of law between nations, such as the International Court of Justice, would have been seen as worthy developments in promoting world peace.

The 1987 achievement of the New Zealand Nuclear Free Zone, Disarmament, and Arms Control Act was a cause for celebration. New Zealand became the first and only country in the western alliance to legislate a nuclear-free zone, for which it was expelled from the Australian, New Zealand and United States (ANZUS) Treaty. This accomplishment would have overjoyed Norman Murray Bell. He would have enjoyed the Oxford Union debate two years earlier, on the proposition that "Nuclear Weapons are Morally Indefensible," between the affirmative team led by New Zealand Prime Minister David Lange (1942-2005) and the negative team led by American Moral Majority founder Jerry Falwell (1933-2007), which was won convincingly by the affirmative side, with David Lange's memorable quip, "I can smell the uranium on [your breath] as you lean towards me."[32] He did not live to see Christchurch become New Zealand's first Peace City in 2002, or receive the New Zealand World Peace Bell in 2005, much as he would have been gratified by their occurrence. But his life had made an enduring contribution towards the realisation of those events. However, recent world events have been cause for dismay: at the end of the cold war the American and Russian nuclear arsenals were reduced by about 90 per cent, but recently a new nuclear arms race has broken out.

In terms of later twentieth-century theology, we can safely assume that Norman Murray Bell would have readily explored the ideas of the Jesus Seminar. Founded in 1985 by American New Testament scholars, it soon gained an international following for its quest for the authentic voice of the historical Jesus.

Chapter 5

Rev. Professor Sir Lloyd Geering being presented with insignia of a Member of the Order of New Zealand by Governor General Anand Satyanand in 2007

Bell would have also been strongly attracted to the theology expounded by Lloyd Geering, one of New Zealand's best known public intellectuals. Sometimes called the prophet of modernity, a biographer has pointed out that

> He called for a return to "prophetic ministry" and advocated that the preacher must be both a scholar of the word of God and of the secular world in which we all live. His life's work has been to embody this, preaching the findings of modern science and thought and evolving a religious world view to encompass this new knowledge.[33]

Professor Geering has written extensively about the impact of the environmental crisis for the future of humanity and the need for a new ethical response: "The continuing life of each species depends upon the preservation of a delicate balance between the organism and the environment that supports it." Elsewhere he has said it is that the "ecosphere itself is in the process of being resanctified. The loving care of Mother Earth, and all which that involves, is to a large extent replacing the former sense of obedience to the Heavenly Father."[34] Norman Murray Bell would have embraced this new ethic in countering the unprecedented challenge to the survival of human civilisation. By the same token, he would have seen how perilous the threat is and how bleak the outlook for success, especially as once again the most powerful nation, the United States of America, was resiling from an earlier commitment to mitigate the effects of climate change until the election of a new President in 2021.

The Plowshares Movement, founded on Christian principles, would have also attracted him, through its active resistance to nuclear weapons. Begun in America in 1980 with the support of the Catholic Worker Movement, it takes its name from the prophecy in Isaiah 2:4: "they shall beat their swords into plowshares, and their spears into pruning hooks: nation shall not lift up sword against nation, neither shall they learn war anymore." There may have been a dilemma for Norman Murray Bell here as the Plowshares Movement accepts that destruction of property, usually military, is justified because of the risk to the survival of humanity entailed in the use of nuclear weapons. For his part, Bell did not engage in property damage, although in this case, he may have made an exception. As it spread around the world the Movement was no longer exclusively Christian in character, embracing supporters from all faiths and none. In 2008 Plowshares activists entered a secure communication base near Blenheim, New Zealand, damaging part of the facility. (The facility is part of the Five Eyes allied intelligence gathering system.) The three men stood trial in Wellington and were found not guilty.

Norman Murray Bell saw the issues of poverty, economic inequality, racial prejudice, gender inequality, protection of minorities, international peace and environmental justice through the lens of religious social ethics. On the world stage, the removal of colonialism had long been one of his goals. The era following World War II saw the end of European empires: by 1965 over 40 countries in Africa and Asia, which included a quarter of the world's population, had become independent. In New Zealand he would have welcomed and supported the formation of the Treaty of Waitangi Tribunal in 1975 to hear Māori claims of injustice from the time of European colonisation and to provide settlement recommendations to the government. Forty years on the Tribunal has received over 2,000 claims. Most have been settled with transfer of resources, cultural redress and official apologies. Successive

Chapter 5

governments have ensured that the impetus of the settlement process is maintained.

And he would have welcomed the stance taken by advocates of a revitalised social gospel in the second half of the twentieth century, such as the Rev. Dr Martin Luther King Jr, the great advocate of non-violent civil disobedience in pursuit of civil rights. A hallmark of Dr King's ministry was that he saw the humanity in those who opposed civil rights even when they refused to see the common humanity in him. On many occasions, he included in his speeches the words "The arc of the moral universe is long, but it bends toward justice." [35] Following Dr King's assassination the torch was passed to the Rev. Dr William Barber II, founder of the Poor People's Campaign: A National Call for a Moral Revival, named in honour of Martin Luther King Jr.

Vegetarianism and animal welfare had been an integral part of Norman Murray Bell's pacifism for thirty years. He continued an advertising campaign for many years in the newspapers against the slaughter of domestic animals for human consumption; under the heading "One World Family of Life No More Slaughter Houses" the text stated: "It is wiser still to regard it as a social duty and an individual privilege, to treat other living beings however they treat you, with understanding, patience and mercy."[36] He ensured that this campaign continued for many years after he died, leaving his estate to pay for monthly advertisements in two local newspapers: one promoting world peace and the other, under the heading "No More Slaughterhouses", to secure peace between humans and domesticated animals. He intended this campaign to run for another thirty years. Subsequent developments in the academic field of animal ethics would have drawn his admiration, though he may well have wondered why it was so long coming: the Rev. Professor Andrew Linzey, an Anglican priest, was appointed to the world's first chair in Ethics, Theology and Animal Welfare at Mansfield College, University of Oxford in 1992. He is the founder and director of the Oxford Centre for Animal Ethics, established in 2006 to promote the study and discussion of animal ethics. Dr Linzey is the first Professor of Animal Ethics at the Graduate Theological Foundation, at Oklahoma City.

When Norman Murray Bell died his voice was un-stilled. He left a greater legacy than his advocacy: he left a legacy of ideas, ideals and an example of self-sacrifice for the good of humanity. Today his name has all but faded from view; no plaque can be found bearing his name, no place records his contribution, no memorial rises to his memory. He is truly a prophet without honour in his own country.

Perhaps the words of T. S. Eliot, from *Four Quartets*, provide a fitting epitaph:

> Time Present and time past
> Are both perhaps present in time future
> And time future contained in time past.
> If all time is eternally present
> All time is unredeemable.[37]

Afterword

Larry Ross and Nuclear-Free New Zealand

Lawrence Frederick James Ross (1927-2012), known as Larry, lived from the age of eight in Toronto, Canada, where he studied engineering and business at the University of Toronto. While at university, as the world faced the threat of nuclear war, he joined the Unitarian Church and embraced the philosophy of peace. This led to his involvement with peace activities that would eventually bring him to New Zealand. There his lifelong dedication to peace work made a significant contribution to the adoption of New Zealand's nuclear free policy. In New Zealand, wide recognition of his peace work included official honours from government and civic authorities, as well as receiving the award of Humanist of the Year.

Larry continued his involvement with Unitarian and Humanist organisations throughout his adulthood. He died in Christchurch on 18 April 2012. This examination of his life seeks to bring into focus the importance of these underpinnings as a source for his ethical worldview.

Education and Unitarianism

Larry Ross was the youngest of five children, born at Yonkers, a suburb of New York City, on 25 November 1927. When he was eight years old, his father retired as an advertising executive and the family moved to Toronto in Ontario, Canada. There he attended a prestigious independent school affiliated with the University of Toronto, the University of Toronto Day School, which was established in 1910. It followed a specialised curriculum and its enhanced teaching methods produced

Afterword

many students who would go on to achieve success at university and their careers later in life.

By the end of World War II Larry had completed his schooling and entered the University of Toronto, where he studied Engineering and Business in the Engineering Faculty for three years and completed a professional engineering degree. During his time at university Larry became involved with the Unitarian Church and began taking an interest the threat that atomic weapons posed to human survival. He had been deeply affected by seeing photographs of the effects of the atomic bomb destruction of Hiroshima. His interest in Unitarianism arose from an intellectual quest rather than family background: both of his grandfathers were ministers, one Baptist and the other Methodist. They did, however, share a concern about social issues, which was passed on to Larry's parents and eventually to him.

The First Unitarian Congregation of Toronto, which Larry joined in the late 1940s, had been reinvigorated with the recent appointment of the Rev. Bill Jenkins (1911-1985), a religious humanist active in social issues.[1] The views of this radical clergyman would chime with Larry's own, especially concerning the origins of the universe and human evolution and the rejection of religious mythology. As Larry put it, "From the age of 16 on I questioned the authenticity of the Christian stories. I came to the conclusion that they weren't true and that they were more of a myth."[2]

Larry chaired a group at the Toronto Unitarian church which examined Cold War topics. In the early 1950s the group invited Corliss Lamont (1903-1995), Professor of Philosophy at Columbia University, to visit the Toronto church. Lamont was a peace campaigner and author of the seminal volume *The Philosophy of Humanism*, first published in 1949, which included the *Humanist Manifesto,* initiated by Unitarian ministers and endorsed by other humanists in 1933. In his Oxford days Lamont had roomed with Julian Huxley, author of *Religion Without Revelation* — another influential writer at the time the young Larry was undergoing his intellectual development. Unfortunately Lamont was denied a passport by the United States Department of State from 1951 to 1958. This was in retaliation for the stand Lamont took against the communist smear tactics of Senator Joseph McCarthy, which resulted

Young Larry Ross

in his being convicted of contempt of Congress. Without a passport Professor Lamont was unable to make the visit.

Later Larry would describe his philosophy as ethical humanism. As an ethical humanist, he explained, "We have to learn to live together ... as a human race, that's the only chance we've got, we can terminate it, therefore it is our job if we value this life and the future of the species we will do something to preserve it and that's why I'm doing what I'm doing to try to preserve the species. Really that's what it boils down to, as an ethical humanist." He saw Jesus as a good leader and an ethical man: "His examples are of value to everybody, we don't throw them away but we look at them in a new light. And we'd like to promote that. That Christ was not the son of God but he was an enlightened leader."[3]

Peace Activities, Marriage and Family

Two other important events happened in Larry's life while he was at university. He became increasingly concerned about the threat to human life from atomic weapons, which he saw as "mutual suicide and extermination",[4] and he identified with the moral principles expounded

Afterword

by Albert Schweitzer (1875-1965). A doyen in Unitarian circles, Schweitzer was awarded the Nobel Prize for Peace in 1952. At the award ceremony in 1954 he delivered his Nobel Lecture entitled "The Problem of Peace", with an authoritative anti-war message. War must be rejected for ethical reasons, he declared, because war makes us all guilty of the crime of inhumanity. In April 1957 Schweitzer broadcast his speech "Declaration of Conscience", in which he pointed to the dangers of radioactivity, uranium and the hydrogen bomb on all living things, and called for all experiments with atom bombs to end. The Declaration was broadcast on radio in over fifty countries and translated into many languages. In the United States it was not broadcast and appeared in only one publication: *The Saturday Review*, whose editor, Norman Cousins, was a peace activist.

In the United States Schweitzer's views were officially labelled communist propaganda and the harmful effects of radiation on health were denied. Schweitzer was on a blacklist: state institutions were instructed not to send him birthday greetings and the government opposed Princeton awarding him an honorary doctorate. Schweitzer never returned to the United States. The situation only improved under President Kennedy, who entered into the first Partial Test Ban Treaty, of which Schweitzer approved. Then he was no longer *persona non grata*. In 1962 Schweitzer became a life member of the Unitarian Universalist Church of the Larger Fellowship.[5] He worked with Bertrand Russell seeking the abolition of nuclear weapons. So it was understandable that Larry was attracted to his philosophy and activism and joined the Albert Schweitzer Peace group.

The second important event involved Larry's private life: he met Sylvia Faith Taylor, a philosophy student. They married in 1948 and she completed her MA while carrying their first baby. They had three children, Laurel (known as Laurie), Gregory and Katherine. Larry worked as a time and methods industrial engineer for the next five years. Following the hospitalisation of Sylvia with a severe psychiatric illness, Larry decided in 1956 to move with the children to Montreal, where he changed his career and became an advertising executive. In Montreal he met and later married Shirley Richardson. Shirley became stepmother to the three children from his first marriage. Shirley and Larry would also have three children, Mark and twins April and Darrell. Interested in natural home birth, Larry developed a skill using hypnosis and was able to help Shirley with pain control during childbirth.

Larry was active in the Lakeshore Unitarian Universalist Congregation, led by its minister, Charles Eddis. With Montreal on the missile path between the Soviet Union and New York, Larry was becoming increasingly concerned about the Cold War: the risk of confrontation between the two superpowers, America and Russia, and the threat of nuclear war. The American government was telling its citizens to build nuclear fallout shelters in their back yards in order to survive an attack, something Larry thought was absurd: "If you did happen to survive a few weeks you'd watch your children die slowly if not from disease, radiation or from starvation or from barbarism with the warring tribes that might arise out of the nuclear wasteland..."[6]

Both Larry and Shirley worked assiduously in peace groups: Shirley was active in Voice of Women and they were members of World Federalists of Canada, a group advocating global peace through world government and an international police force. As international tension continued to mount, the General Assembly of the United Nations passed resolution 1653 in November 1961, declaring that the use of nuclear weapons violated the United Nations Charter, was contrary to international law and constituted a crime against humanity. Larry and Shirley made the decision to move with the children to the most distant country they could find in the Southern Hemisphere with a democratic system and first-world standard of living.

A Sanctuary in New Zealand

Before Larry and Shirley arrived in New Zealand as nuclear refugees from the northern hemisphere, others had imagined how this antipodean sanctuary could ensure the survival of flora following a northern nuclear war. Steps had been taken decades earlier to preserve northern hemisphere plant life, which otherwise was likely to be destroyed, at Eastwoodhill, New Zealand's national arboretum on the east coast of the North Island. It contains the largest collection of Northern Hemisphere trees and shrubs growing in the Southern Hemisphere. Established in 1918, it had undergone considerable expansion following

Afterword

the end of World War II because of the potential catastrophe posed by nuclear war.[7] There were also scientific concerns about the risk to New Zealand of a "nuclear winter" following a northern war. It was thought that even a small decrease in the New Zealand temperature, due to the immense amount of debris that would be ejected into the atmosphere, would cause primary production to reduce significantly.[8] This could potentially decrease the ability of New Zealand to feed its own dependent population.

In May 1962, Larry and Shirley arrived in Auckland with their six children. A month later they both became members of the New Zealand Rationalist Association.[9] Larry's interest in humanism, which began in Canada, grew with his admiration of the stand taken by Bertrand Russell against nuclear weapons. Larry said: "Bertrand Russell has always been my favourite philosopher. I corresponded with him on war [and] peace issues from Canada in 1961 and continued from New Zealand in 1962 on the Vietnam War."[10] In addition, Russell was a leading figure in the British humanist movement.

Bertrand Russell

After a month touring the North Island the family moved to Christchurch, a city with a peace heritage stretching back before World War I, when the Peace Council was formed by Charles Mackie and Harry Atkinson. How much, if any, of this background was known to Larry when the decision was made to settle in Christchurch is unknown, but the fact that university friends from Montreal had migrated there six months earlier was a consideration.

Now Larry began his anti-nuclear campaign with intense moral clarity and purpose: his determination would come to be seen as his strength by his supporters and obduracy by his detractors. He published "World War III and New Zealand" in the *New Zealand Rationalist*[11] just before the world teetered on the nuclear abyss over the Cuban missile crisis, for thirteen days between 15 and 28 October 1962. In its next issue the *New Zealand Rationalist* followed Larry's article with one by the renowned Unitarian Humanist Linus Pauling (1901-1994), entitled "There is No Alternative to Peace".[12] This was the evidence Pauling was not allowed to give by the Old Bailey Judge at the trial of the six members of the Committee of 100, which saw Bertrand Russell and the other defendants imprisoned for illegal protest activities. Bertrand Russell was a "great man ... an example of what we can become", Larry wrote. "He was willing to act for his principles and go to jail for peace actions at age 90."[13]

Bertrand Russell established his peace foundation in 1963 and a year later he invited Larry to form the Australian and New Zealand branch. Not limited to anti-nuclear activities, the Bertrand Russell Peace Foundation was soon in the forefront of opposition to the Vietnam War. Larry had also joined the United Nations Association of New Zealand and supported its anti-Vietnam War activities. Larry attacked the government's policy with the skill of a seasoned debater, culminating in a written exchange with the Prime Minister and the then Acting Minister of External Affairs. The published debate[14] drew a retort from the Prime Minister Keith Holyoake, claiming that Larry "was not a genuine seeker after truth, and ... nothing I can say, and no assurance I might give, would prevail against his closed mind and fixed ideas."[15] Although by no means receiving equal treatment as the pro-war lobby in mainstream media, Larry's campaign was effective in exposing weaknesses in the official case, as this personal criticism from the Prime Minister indicates. Also in 1963, Larry wrote an "Open Letter to World Statesmen" stating that New Zealand should be surrounded by a nuclear free zone and that such a zone could become the model for future treaties. Following up these ideas in more detail, Larry presented them to the 1964 conference of the United Nations Association of New Zealand. That year he became the subject of a report to the Prime Minister from the Director of the Security Intelligence Service (SIS), giving a warning that:

> Almost immediately after his arrival in New Zealand, ROSS began writing to newspapers. He has continued an incessant barrage of letters and articles ever since. His main theme has been nuclear disarmament and plans for a nuclear free Southern Hemisphere ... ROSS is obsessed with the idea that nuclear war is inevitable in the Northern Hemisphere and with a desire to keep New Zealand out of it.[16]

A further report in 1965 from the Director of SIS to the Prime Minister stated that Larry was chairman of the Bertrand Russell Peace Foundation, noting: "He has produced a flood of Foundation literature; all of it prepared by himself, condemning US policy in Vietnam." It added that Larry had not been in paid employment since he arrived three years earlier. With some accuracy the report said he seemed to have "ample private funds to continue his present unpaid preoccupation with 'peace' [sic] matters...".[17] What it does not say is that funding for Larry's three years of full-time unpaid work came from a legacy from his father. Nor, rather surprisingly, does it mention that his political activities were entirely peaceful and lawful. At this time Larry was the primary driver of Christchurch opposition to the Vietnam War, ramping up the level of activity when he formed the Citizens Vietnam Action Committee in 1967.

Larry remained chairman of the Bertrand Russell Peace Foundation until 1968, although the Foundation continued until 1975. In 1969 Larry discovered that his family commitments required a full-time breadwinner. He found a job as sales manager for a local building society. While his employment curtailed his peace activities, it did not eliminate them altogether. As the tide of public opinion began to turn against the Vietnam War in the United States and many of its allies, demonstrations began in New Zealand in April 1970. Christchurch saw 1000 demonstrators in Cathedral Square, while a student rally at Canterbury University attended by 500 people listened to speeches from Murray Horton, Larry Ross and James K. Baxter (1926-1972), interspersed with rock music.

In 1978 Larry applied to become a New Zealand citizen, which required a SIS evaluation. The report noted that his political activity was largely directed against the Vietnam War, which did not fall within the Government's Cabinet Directive on Citizenship. So the official response was "No Comment", with a handwritten note on the file stating: "I think ROSS is a minimal current interest."[18] Larry subsequently held New Zealand and Canadian dual citizenship. He continued to work full time until 1980, when he retired to form the New Zealand Nuclear Free Zone Association. He was already supporting the Humanist Peace Fellowship New Zealand, which was active between 1979 and 1985; it aided the Students and Teachers Organisation for Peace, peace forums, and maintained links with the international humanist peace movement.[19]

The Nuclear Free Zone Campaign

In October 1981, at the Annual Peace Conference at Living Springs, Christchurch, attended by people from around the country, Larry presented a five-point plan to achieve a nuclear free New Zealand. The idea was based on the United Nations resolutions that nation states should declare themselves nuclear weapons free zones in order to promote world disarmament. Larry included the principle of "positive" neutrality in the plan, that is, the idea that a nuclear free New Zealand would not be isolationist but would advocate positive peace-making neutrality. It would offer peace-making services to countries facing conflict. The plan also called for the modification of the ANZUS (Australian, New Zealand and United States) Treaty so that United States ships or aircraft carrying nuclear weapons could be prevented from entering New Zealand territory.

By December 1981 Larry had formed the New Zealand Nuclear Free Zone Committee. It focussed on public education regarding the threat of the nuclear arms race and the necessity of completely excluding nuclear weapons or warships. Larry designed advertising materials that

Afterword

would identify the peace movement, including the logo, badges, posters and stickers. He produced the merchandise using these designs which was sold and used by peace groups throughout the country. Larry coordinated the campaign around the country: he published the Nuclear Free newsletter, held meetings, travelled around New Zealand promoting local peace groups and getting them to lobby their local authority or council to declare their area a nuclear free zone. His first national lecture tour was in March 1982. He held that the lobbying of local Members of Parliament was vital. The increasing groundswell of public support was shown in the letters and petitions, which Larry ensured reached the Parliamentarians.

The Nuclear Free organisation was unable to pay Larry for the work he did, though he did earn a modest amount from the sale of merchandise. But the full-time commitment to peace work came at a personal cost: his marriage to Shirley broke down and they separated, and divorced in 1983. Larry also revealed that there were times when he wished he had been a better father to his children. It came down to giving them more time: "I could have been there more," he said.[20] In the 1990s he formed a deep relationship with Brenda Crocker, whom he introduced to his Unitarian friends, and they enjoyed many aspects of life together until he died.

Success came with the election of the Labour government led by David Lange (1942-2005) in 1984 with its nuclear free policy, virtually the same as that of the peace movement. The new government announced that the visit of a United States warship, the USS *Buchanan*, would not be welcome. The United States then suspended its treaty obligations to New Zealand under the ANZUS alliance. The British foreign minister Baroness Janet Young arrived, carrying a large black umbrella, on a visit to admonish Lange and try to get him to change his mind. The mission failed and Lange was heard to say "she'd left her broomstick in my office."[21]

Three years later the Labour government was re-elected and passed the New Zealand Nuclear Free Zone, Disarmament and Arms Control Act 1987, under which all of its territorial sea, land and air-space became nuclear free zones. It represented over a decade's effort by the peace movement, churches, trade unions, the Labour Party, and two minor parties: the New Zealand Democrats and the Values Party, later the Green Party.[22] By the time the Act was passed there were 105 local councils covering nearly three-quarters of the population that had been declared nuclear free zones. Prime Minister David Lange acknowledged the effectiveness of the nuclear free zone campaign: "One of [the peace groups'] goals was to have local authorities declare their territory to be a nuclear-free zone. In this, they were largely successful." He pointed out that by the time of the 1984 general election many local bodies were nuclear free, and while skeptics could sneer at their impracticality "their educative effect was great."[23] There was international opposition, led by the United States, to the "New Zealand disease" which enshrined a nation's nuclear weapons and/or propulsion free policy into legislation. At home popular support was now enormous: polls showed over 90 per cent of the population supported the law.

The Nuclear Free Peacemaking Association formed by Larry in 1988 grew out of the New Zealand Nuclear Free Zone Committee. The change Larry brought about signalled his desire to see foreign and

Larry Ross with the logo he designed for Nuclear Free New Zealand

Afterword

Stuart Macaskill

defence policies which complemented the nuclear free legislation of 1987, including international peace-making, neutrality and withdrawal from military alliances.[24] The new direction involved both education and political lobbying: tours around the country with internationally known speakers, public lectures about the horror of nuclear war, and overseas travel to encourage other countries to become nuclear weapons free. He visited Australia, Italy, Japan and Canada. At home Larry organised lobbying and deputations to Members of Parliament, media interviews and approaches to local councils seeking reaffirmation of their nuclear free status. This campaign was conducted under the slogan "Keep New Zealand Nuclear Free." It protected and built upon the legislative gains made and brought New Zealand onto the international stage again. A century before it had been known as the social laboratory of the world; now it was known as the peace-making laboratory of the world. This international leadership continued when Stuart Macaskill (1931-2012), President of Local Government New Zealand, at the 1995 International Union of Local Authorities conference in The Hague, called on France to stop nuclear testing in the Pacific. The initiative for this action came from the groundswell of nuclear free zones amongst

New Zealand local authorities. The resolution, seconded by Australia, passed unanimously. It was the first time this international body had taken a political stance on a global issue. This added pressure appeared to be effective, as the last French nuclear test occurred in the Pacific in the following year.

After the success of the Nuclear-Free New Zealand campaign, Larry continued to oppose war when it occurred in various places, including the Gulf War in 1991, the invasion of Afghanistan in 2001, and the occupation of Iraq in 2003.

More Unitarian Involvement and Enjoying Life

Larry and Brenda found more time for travel and relaxation. Hanmer Springs was enjoyable for swimming and soaking in the hot pools. Larry loved going on camping trips with comfortable beds. At the age of 75 he was still snow skiing. Larry and Brenda travelled around Britain and Canada with the help of a peace and travel group, Servas, which provided a network of hosts for travellers to help build world peace. In Canada the colours of trees in the fall were lovely. Later, another trip took them to Western Australia for a month. There they photographed the varied and beautiful flora. It was only the imposition of health problems that curtailed their travels.

In December 1995, Larry joined the steering committee chaired by Derek McCullough, which established the Unitarian Universalist Fellowship of Christchurch. Larry was already in contact with the New Zealand Society of Unitarians, having published his "Open Letter to New Zealand Members of Parliament and Citizens" in their journal *Motive*.[25]

In 1998 Larry visited the Marlborough Unitarian Fellowship, which had been established in 1988 by two retired ministers: Elspeth Rosalind Vallance (née Hall, 1915-2009) and her husband Arthur Woolley Vallance (1902-1990), who had married in 1939. Arthur won a scholarship to Lincoln College, Oxford, read Modern History, graduated in 1924 and entered Manchester College, Oxford to study for the Unitarian ministry. Elspeth went to St Anne's College, Oxford, in 1933 where she studied history. She graduated with a BA degree in 1936 and entered Manchester College, Oxford to study theology

Afterword

Elspeth Vallance

for the Unitarian ministry. While at St Anne's she attended a series of lectures Albert Schweitzer gave at Manchester College in 1934.[26] She was very impressed with his message and later met him at a reception in the College Library. Arthur and Elspeth had a number of ministries in the North of England which extended over 40 years,[27] often with Elspeth acting as Arthur's assistant. At his church in Salford, Arthur formed the Albert Schweitzer Boys' Club. Arthur was President of the General Assembly of Unitarian and Free Christian Churches in 1959-60. After their retirement Arthur and Elspeth decided to follow a son to Blenheim, Marlborough, New Zealand in 1987. Elspeth wrote that "Albert Schweitzer, our 20th century saint whom I look upon as a great guru for the present and the future, gave us the watchwords Reverence for Life."[28] In Elspeth and Arthur Vallance, Larry found two likeminded people who were also motivated by the Schweitzerian principles concerning peace and opposition to war. When Larry visited Marlborough he mounted a display of his peace work and spoke about it.

Larry gave the address at the third Christchurch Fellowship service in April 1996. In August 1999 his subject was "The Universe — Human Nature, Extinction and Survival". In August 2000 he spoke on "The

Growing Threat of Creationism and Fundamentalism". In May 2001 his subject was "New Zealand Defence in a Nuclear Age". In September 2002 his address was on "Effective Prayer without God". In March 2004 the topic was "The Dangers of Fundamentalist Beliefs on George Bush, American Policy and Islam". Larry believed that George W. Bush had an apocalyptic worldview based on Christian fundamentalism: it entailed a war between Muslims and Jews which would bring about the Second Coming of Christ, a *folie a deux* the Christian Right shared with extremist religious Jews. Larry argued that for a president "mentally armed with the Christian Fundamentalist religion, anything is possible and everything can be divinely justified."[29] Larry thought that the Bush administration had become a bigger threat to world peace than terrorists and that the strategy it devised, of war on terror, was counter-productive.

On other occasions the two Fellowships held joint residential retreats at Kaikoura on the Takahanga Marae, which Larry enjoyed. Elspeth Vallance became minister emeritus for the South Island of New Zealand in 2003 at a service attended by Marlborough and Christchurch Unitarians. Derek McCullough was appointed minister in training for the South Island. He completed his training in 2006 and was covenanted as Minister to the Unitarian Universalist Fellowship of Christchurch. Both positions strengthened the regional Unitarian organisations.

Derek McCullough

Afterword

In April 2005 Larry gave his last address at the Christchurch fellowship on "The Danger of a Global Hiroshima". Following Larry's service in 2005 he began experiencing health problems and did not lead other services, although he continued to attend meetings. His last attendance was on All Heretics Day,[30] 1 April 2012, a few weeks before he died. The funeral service was taken by his friend Derek McCullough, the Unitarian Universalist Minister.

Public recognition for Larry's enormous voluntary contribution to peace work was forthcoming, first with the award of the Queen's Service Medal in 1987. This was followed with the New Zealand Humanist of the Year Peace Award in 1988.[31] He received the Christchurch Peace City Award in 2002. In 2012 he received the Lifetime Peacemaker Award from the New Zealand Peace Foundation. Posthumously, Larry was recognised when the Larry Ross Nuclear Free New Zealand Peace Memorial Park bench was installed 24 April 2016, on the banks of the Avon River, Christchurch.

Mayor of Christchurch awarding Larry Ross the Christchurch Peace City award, 2002

Acknowledgements

Information has been located in a number of repositories within New Zealand and overseas. In New Zealand, images and archival information about Dr James Bell and his wife Henrietta, grandparents of Norman Murray Bell, were made available by Peter Marsh, Curator/Manager at the Albertland and Districts Museum at Wellsford. Mr Marsh found uncatalogued information about members of the Bell family and other Albertland settlers, providing important details about this early period of the Bell family in New Zealand.

Secondary schooling details and academic achievements were provided by Jane Teal, archivist of Christ's College, Christchurch. University of New Zealand academic records of Norman Murray Bell's studies at Canterbury College were provided by Wendy Robinson, Portfolio Manager-Academic Programmes Universities New Zealand, Wellington. The curator-archivist of Christchurch Boys High School, Dr Bruce Harding, kindly found the issue of the school magazine containing news of Norman Murray Bell's appointment to the teaching staff in 1916.

A substantial collection of his writings, photographs and other memorabilia was donated to the Christchurch Public Library by a relative following Norman Murray Bell's death. This trove includes *A Gospel of Universal Compassion Being Another Side of Christianity*, *Education for Freedom*, and *Maori Myths and Rites in the Light of Human Ontogeny*. Another copy of the last-named document, with 18 extra pages, is held

Acknowledgements

in the MacMillan Brown Library of the University of Canterbury, where it is described as: Bell, N. M (Norman Murray), *Maori myths and rites in the light of human ontogeny: a physiologic[o]-psychical contribution to the study of religious origins*. D. Litt. Thesis, Canterbury University College, 1928. Unfortunately the University of Canterbury has decided not to provide this thesis to researchers on the usual basis theses are made available, certainly within the English speaking world, namely digitalised format transmitted to the borrowing library. After agreeing to send it but failing to provide a copy to Auckland Public Libraries, for over a year Massey University Library sought and expected a copy from the University of Canterbury. No explanation was forthcoming for this limited form of censorship, although the thesis can be read at the University of Canterbury Library. This is particularly unhelpful when an evaluation of Norman Murray Bell's magnum opus is needed to understand this work and the context within which it was created.

More of Norman Murray Bell's material appears to be held by relatives. What is already in the public domain has a dearth of his diaries, journals, letters and other personal records. While it may have arisen from a failure to examine and sort through the material, there is always the risk of posthumous privacy being exercised in the belief, however well intentioned, of protecting the memory of a family member. This lacuna limits our understanding of the man and his motivations. It may perhaps spring from a viewpoint, glimpsed at in the available record, where Norman Murray Bell is shown in moments of relaxation and holiday, often bicycling, in male company and that he remained single. While this may be of no significance whatsoever, such reticence has no place in today's society and ought not to be a barrier in allowing us a balanced appreciation of the man.

Norman Murray Bell published *Cosmos: A Quarterly Journal of Pacifist Thought* on a regular basis between 1934 and 1942. He contributed two long articles to the intellectual magazine *Tomorrow*: one on Christianity, the other on the use of the wireless (radio), then a comparatively new device, for public education. The Canterbury Museum in Christchurch holds correspondence between Norman Murray Bell and Charles Mackie, the Baptist lay preacher who was the principal founding member of the National Peace Council.[1]

Acknowledgements

A smaller collection of Bell's material is found in the Alexander Turnbull Library, part of the National Library of New Zealand, in Wellington. The record of Bell's military service, Court Martials and imprisonment was obtained from the New Zealand Government Archives. There is a small collection of *Cosmos* in the General Assembly Library of the New Zealand Parliament.

Important overseas material was obtained from archives in the United Kingdom at Cambridge, Liverpool, London, and St Andrews Universities. Mr Jonathan Smith, Archivist and Modern Manuscript Cataloguer, Trinity College Library, University of Cambridge provided information about Norman Murray Bell's academic record and achievements. Mr Richard Temple, archivist at University of London, was very helpful finding information about the religious studies undertaken by Norman Murray Bell.

On the continent, Heidelberg University provided a useful response and Bern University provided a copy of Norman Murray Bell's record. In addition, the British Library provided important information about the Theistic Church, founded by the former Anglican priest Charles Voysey, and the Free Religious Movement into which it evolved, under the leadership of Dr Walter Walsh and subsequently Will Hayes. The archives of Harris Manchester College at the University of Oxford hold an important cache of letters from Voysey at the time he established the Theistic Church, copies of which were kindly provided by Sue Killoran, Fellow Librarian. Dr Williams Library in London has a collection of the writings of Charles Voysey and his successor Walter Walsh, and kindly provided an important reference to the establishment of the Theology Faculty at the University of London. In London, Librarians at the Library of the Religious Society of Friends (Quakers) kindly provided material about Voysey's meetings in Manchester, the involvement he had with some members of their community, and copies of some of Will Hayes' material.

Many times I received help from CJ Simmons at Auckland City Library, who unfailingly located the information I sought. Dr Stephen Morrissy began this journey with me and provided valuable input along the way.

Acknowledgements

My friends have been generous in providing their time: David Ross in providing technical assistance, Martin Lewis in obtaining copies from Library holdings, Dean Reynolds and Ross Sutherland in reading drafts, noting corrections and making suggestions. The skill and advice of Lynn Hughes, editor of Blackstone Editions, brought this book to completion. I am grateful to you all.

Appendixes

Appendix 1

Voyages of the Albertland Ships

Ship	Departed	Date of Voyage	Number of Passengers
Matilda Wattenbach	London	29 May 1862 - 8 September 1862	352
Hanover	Gravesend	29 May 1862 - 17 September 1862	336
William Miles	Gravesend	29 July 1862 - 12 November 1862	322
		Total for 1862	*1,010*
Gertrude	Gravesend	4 November 1862 - 9 February 1863	147
Tyburnia	Gravesend	2 June 1863 - 4 September 1863	400
Annie Wilson	Gravesend	30 May 1863 - 19 September 1863	329
Ida Zeigler	London	3 July 1863 - 5 October 1863	115
		Total for 1863	*991*

Voyages of the Albertland Ships

Ship	Departed	Date of Voyage	Number of Passengers
John Duncan	Gravesend	11 October 1863 - 23 January 1864	229
Nimroud	London	10 August 1864 - 18 December 1864	175
		Total for 1864	*404*
Victory	Gravesend	2 September 1864 - 4 January 1865	247
Caduceus	London	30 November 1864 - 26 March 1865	262
		Total for 1865	*509*
		Total	**2,914**

The Matilda Wattenbach *leaving England, 1862*

APPENDIX 2

Map of the Albertland Settlement

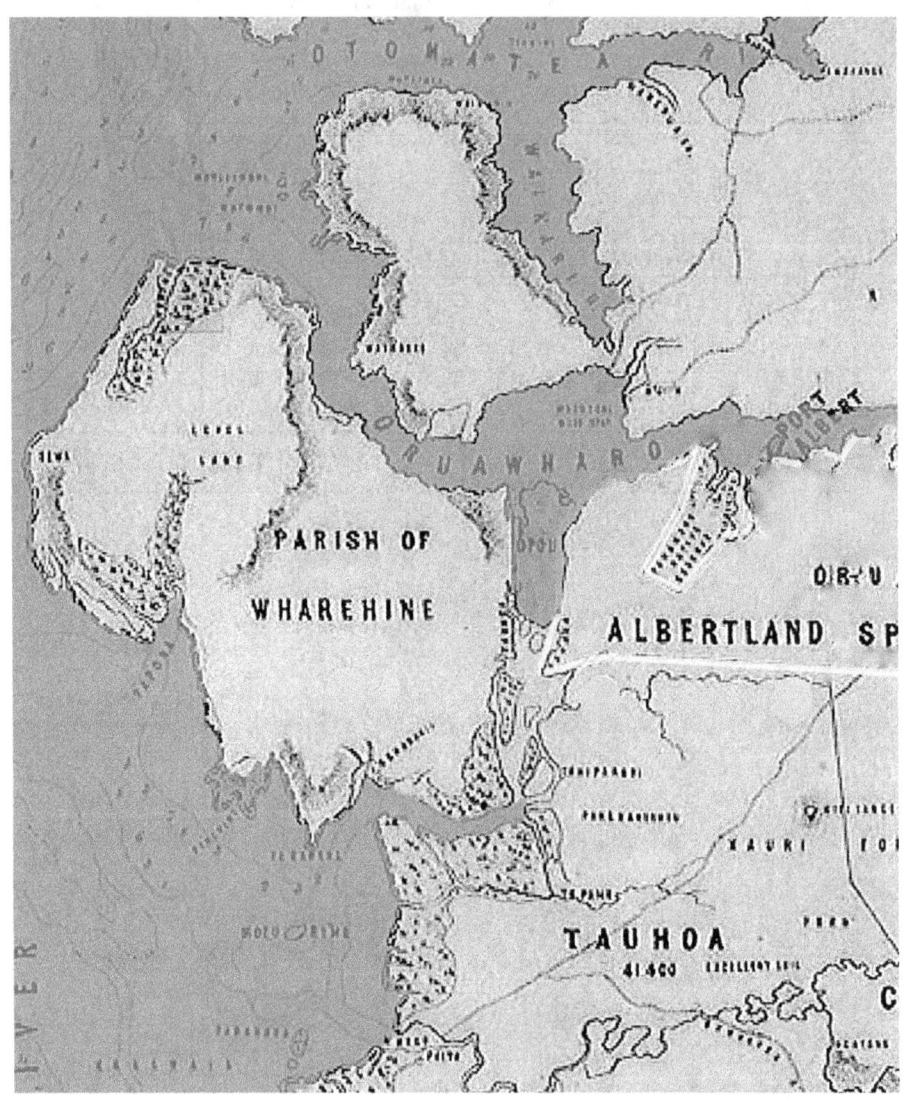

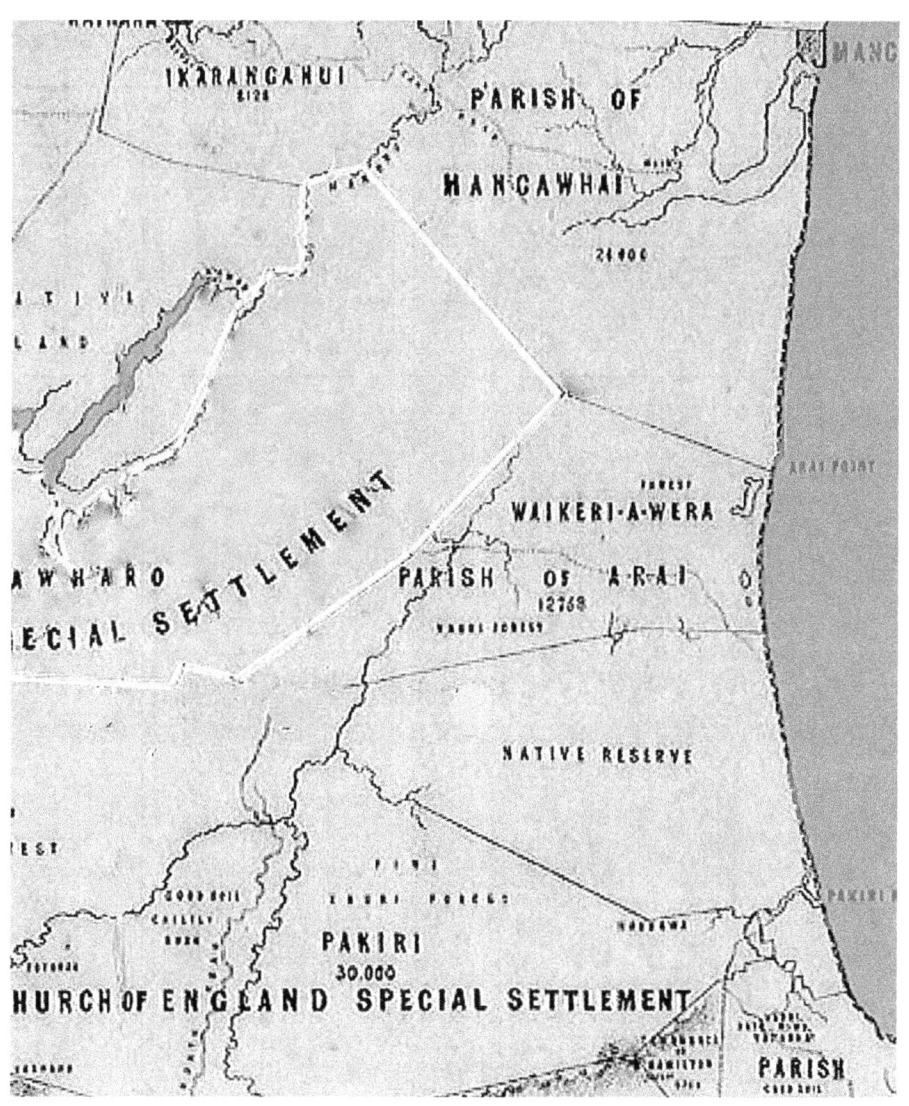

APPENDIX 3
Descendants of James and Henrietta Bell

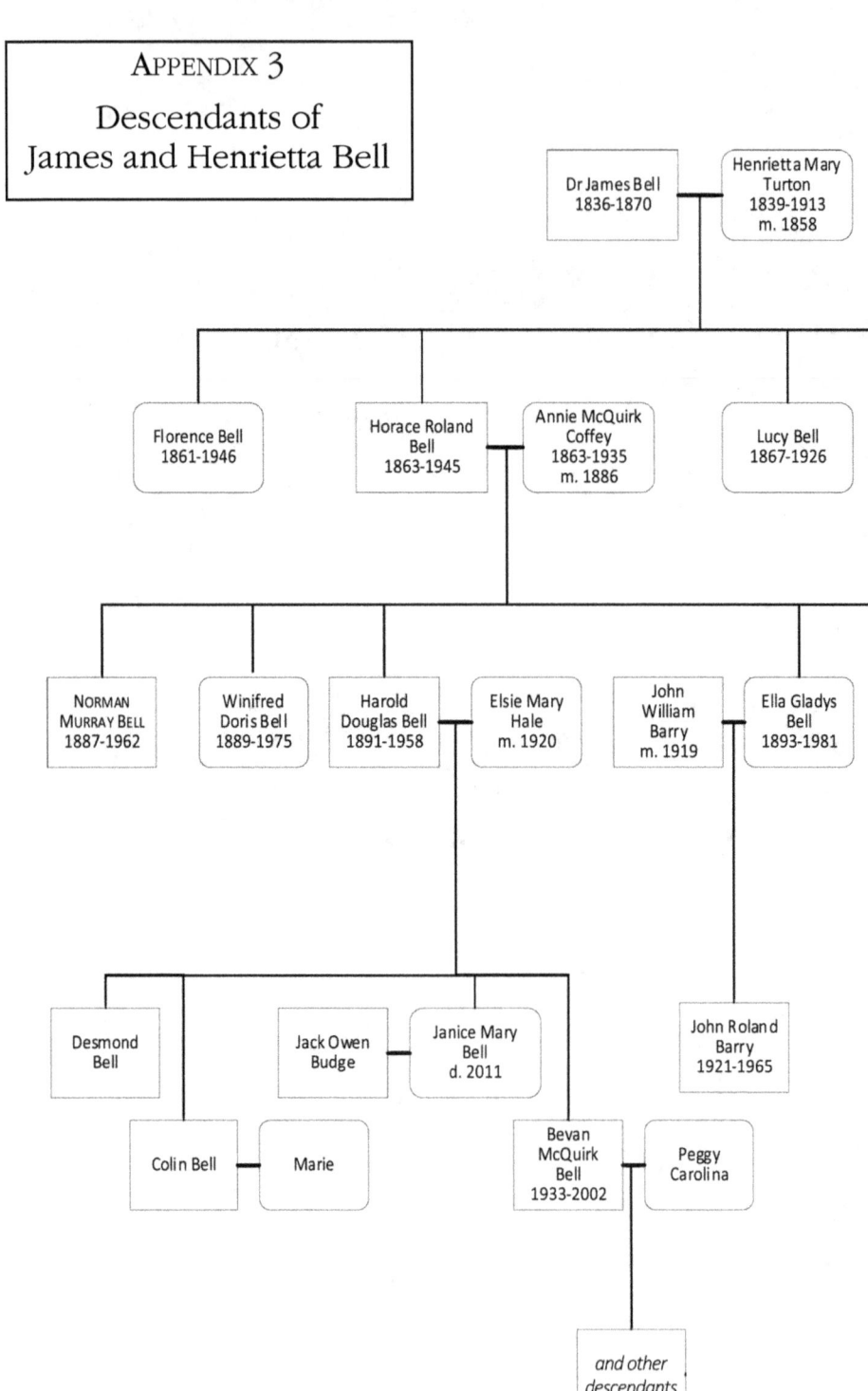

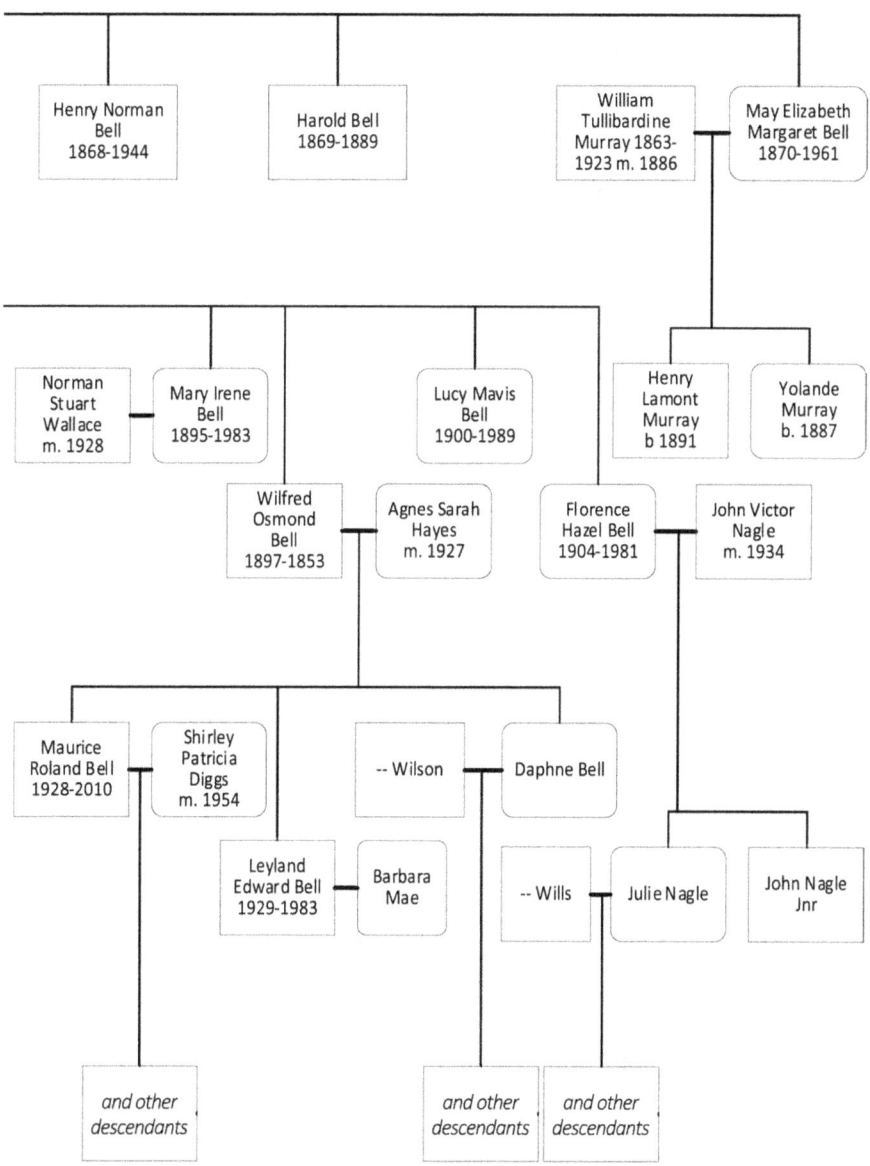

Appendix 4

Free Religious Movement Lectures 1934-1944

Source: *The Press*, advertisements for Sunday Services. Date refers to date of notice published in *The Press*.

Date	Speaker	Topic
26 February 1934	Professor F. Sinclaire	Devotion, the Bible, and Religion
7 April 1934	Professor F. Sinclaire	Not Spoiling our Old Faith
16 April 1934	Mr A. M. Richards	Rising Fascism
29 October 1934	Mr N. M. Bell	Albert Schweitzer, his attitude to Primitive Christianity
17 December 1934	Dr H. D. Broadhead	Aspects of Greek Ethics and Religion
4 April 1936	Mr N. M. Bell	Sevenfold Path to Life
16 May 1936	Mr N. M. Bell	Man's Inhumanity
17 October 1936	Mr N. M. Bell	Cosmic Citizenship
27 March 1937	Mr C. H. Cole	Unrecognised Christs
17 July 1937	Mr C. H. Cole	Defeating Despondency

Free Religious Movement Lectures

Date	Speaker	Topic
24 July 1937	Mr N. M. Bell	Agape (Love) and the Free Religious Movement
10 September 1938	Mr N. M. Bell	What Authority Has Conscience?
25 February 1939	Mr N. M. Bell	Life Though Reconciliation
11 March 1939	Mr N. M. Bell	Food and Love in the Light of Fraternity
18 March 1939	Mr N. M. Bell	Have We Lived Before?
1 April 1939	Mr N. M. Bell	Men and Women, Cosmically
6 May 1939	Mr N. M. Bell	Creative Faith
3 June 1939	Mr N. M. Bell	Are We Worth Defending?
10 June 1939	Mr N. M. Bell	Christian, What Are You Going to Do with that Gun?
17 June 1939	Mr N. M. Bell	Evolution of Ethical Thought on War in the Bible
1 July 1939	Mr N. M. Bell	Biblical Prophecy and Prediction
19 August 1939	Mr N. M. Bell	Is The Whole Universe Alive?
26 August 1939	Mr N. M. Bell	What Does Success in Life Mean?
2 September 1939	Mr N. M. Bell	The Crisis from the Humanitarian Standpoint
9 September 1939	Mr N. M. Bell	Pacifism as a Guide through the Present Crisis
16 September 1939	Mr N. M. Bell	Thou Shalt Do No Murder (except in wartime); or Can You Bayonet your Brother in Love
23 September 1939	Mr N. M. Bell	Can the Genuine Christian Go to War?

Appendix 4

Date	Speaker	Topic
7 October 1939	Mr N. M. Bell	Prayer and War
14 October 1939	Mr N. M. Bell	Can You Serve God through Mammon?
21 October 1939	Mr N. M. Bell	What is the Place of Death in the Scheme of Life?
28 October 1939	Mr N. M. Bell	Freud and the Aggressive Instinct in Man
4 November 1939	Mr N. M. Bell	Does the World Want a New Leader?
11 November 1939	Mr N. M. Bell	Justice Without Love is Injustice
16 December 1939	Mr N. M. Bell	Have I Learnt Anything Vital During 1939?
13 January 1940	Mrs Harvey	Wake Up and Live!
20 January 1940	(Not stated)	Heaven Now and Here
27 January 1940	Mrs Smallwood	Conditions of Life Today
17 February 1940	Mr N. M. Bell	Thou Shalt Not Kill — Love One Another
9 March 1940	Mr D. D. Moffitt	Why Wage War Against Our Brothers?
13 April 1940	Mr N. M. Bell	They're Human, Aren't They?
27 April 1940	Mr N. M. Bell	Are We Seeking a City that We Shall Never Find?
4 May 1940	Mr. C. F. Saunders	The Poverty of Philosophy
11 May 1940	Mr N. M. Bell	Understanding, Forgiveness, Love
18 May 1940	Mr Stewart Kingan	Science and Religion

Free Religious Movement Lectures

Date	Speaker	Topic
25 May 1940	Mr N. M. Bell	The Only Thing that Really Matters
6 July 1940	Mr N. M. Bell	Man in the Making
13 July 1940	Mr B. R. McLaren	Philosophy! What is the Use of It?
10 August 1940	Mr N. M. Bell	Freedom is Good: Equality is Better: Fraternity is Best
17 August 1940	Mr C. F. Saunders	China's Gethsemane
31 August 1940	Mr N. M. Bell	From Piety to Love
21 September 1940	Mr John Johnson	Christianity versus The State
30 November 1940	Sergeant-Major D. D. Moffatt	Mortal Sin
14 December 1940	Mr J. L. B. Pope	The Eternal Xmas
25 January 1941	Mr N. M. Bell	Blessed Are Ye Poor
22 February 1941	Mr N. M. Bell	A Lesson from Goethe
15 March 1941	Mr E. G. Beardsley	Man, Ethics, and Society
12 April 1941	Mr N. M. Bell	The Real Resurrection
3 May 1941	Mr N. M. Bell	Positive: the Religion of Humanity
5 July 1941	Mr J. C. Harding	Spiritualism and the Modern World
2 August 1941	Mr J. L. B. Pope Mr Lightfoot	The Will to Peace (7.00 pm) Dictatorship v. Democracy (8.00 pm)

Appendix 4

Date	Speaker	Topic
11 October 1941	Mr Morse	A Modern Application of the Parable of the Vineyard (Sunday) Social Problems (Wednesday)
22 November 1941	Mr J. Sewell Mr Jones	Philosophy of Omar Khayyam (Sunday) Discussion Group (Wednesday)
29 November 1941	Mrs J. Summers (Connie Jones)	Prison Reform (Sunday) Open Discussion (Wednesday)
24 January 1942	Mr J. L. B. Pope	Ourselves and the New World
28 February 1942	Mr N. M. Bell	Religion and Science
21 March 1942	Miss Trott	The Three Religions of Japan
28 March 1942	Mr N. M. Bell	World Teachers: Epictetus
4 April 1942	Mr N. M. Bell	The Resurrection (combined meeting of Rationalist Association and Free Religious Movement)
24 April 1942	Mr E. G. Beardsley	War and After
2 May 1942	Mr N. M. Bell	Lesson from Goethe's "Faust"
16 May 1942	Mr N. M. Bell	Grab or Share: a Christian Way to End the War
23 May 1942	Mr C. F. Saunders	Open Discussion
11 July 1942	Mr L. C. Walker	Margins in Morality
18 July 1942	Mr N. M. Bell	Parasitism, Biological, Social, Spiritual
1 August 1942	Mr N. M. Bell	The Prophetic Message

Free Religious Movement Lectures

Date	Speaker	Topic
8 August 1942	Mr N. M. Bell	Gandhi, Apostle of Non-Violence
22 August 1942	Mr N. M. Bell	Hindu and Mohammedan
26 September 1942	Mr L. H. Booth Mr Taylor	The Place of Art in Soviet Life (Sunday) Discussion Group (Wednesday)
3 October 1942	Mr N. M. Bell	Salvation
17 October 1942	Mr N. M. Bell	A Peaceful Way of Attain Peace
24 October 1942	Mr E. G. Beardsley Mr Cole	Fascism: Some Aspects and Retrospects (Sunday) Discussion Group (Wednesday)
31 October 1942	Mr N. M. Bell	A Better Man Makes a Better World
7 November 1942	Mr Neville Joyce	The Education of the New Order
21 November 1942	Mr N. M. Bell	Religion and the Better World
5 December 1942	Prof. F. Sinclaire	A Talk on William Law
23 January 1943	Mr J. Morrison	Training for the Life of the Spirit
30 January 1943	Mr N. M. Bell	Samuel Butler's Ideas
6 February 1943	Mr N. M. Bell	From Power to Love or Evolution in the Bible
13 February 1943	Mr L. H. Booth	Life — The Individual and the Community
6 March 1943	Mr N. M. Bell	A Modern Creed
13 March 1943	Mr C. F. Saunders	Socialist Constitution (Sunday) Discussion Group (Wednesday)

Appendix 4

Date	Speaker	Topic
20 March 1943	Mr N. M. Bell	What Should A Free Religious Movement Be Doing Now?
3 April 1943	Mr N. M. Bell	The Life and Work of Moses
10 April 1943	Mr S. Schofield	Towards a New Order
17 April 1943	Mr N. M. Bell	Is Christianity Outgrown?
24 April 1943	Mr L. C. Walker	Adult Educational Travels (Sunday) Discussion Group (Wednesday)
8 May 1943	Mr E. L. Flavell	Other Days — Other Ways (Sunday) Discussion Group (Wednesday)
22 May 1943	Mr E. Wilzek	The Equality of Human Races (Sunday) Discussion Group (Wednesday)
29 May 1943	Mr N. M. Bell	Modern Religious Ideas, No. 2, Universal Understanding
5 June 1943	Mr N. M. Bell	A Parable and its Interpretation
12 June 1943	Mr E. G. Beardsley	Nature of Idealism (Sunday) Discussion Group (Wednesday)
19 June 1943	Mr N. M. Bell	The Wisdom of Socrates
10 July 1943	Mr L. H. Booth Mr Jones	Thinking Creatively (Sunday) Discussion Group (Wednesday)
24 July 1943	Mr F. W. Heal Mrs M. Townend	Aspects of Life, Spiritual and Material (Sunday) Discussion Group (Wednesday)
7 August 1943	Mr N. M. Bell	The Story of Rhodesia
14 August 1943	Mr N. M. Bell	Is This the Best of All Possible Worlds?
28 August 1943	Mr N. M. Bell	The Colour Bar in Africa

Free Religious Movement Lectures

Date	Speaker	Topic
11 September 1943		Open Forum: The Road to Individual Freedom Lies through Racial and Economic Equality and World Brotherhood
2 October 1943	Mrs M. Townend	The Artist — a Story from Tchekov
9 October 1943		Open Discussion: Theme: The Needed Deeds of Social Repentance
23 October 1943		Open Discussion: Our Pacific Neighbours: Australia?
30 October 1943	Mr L. Hollings	The Teachings of Buddha
6 November 1943		Open Discussion: Two Nations Between whom there is no Intercourse: The Rich and the Poor
13 November 1943	Mr N. M. Bell	Our Pacific Neighbours: The Japanese Open Discussion: Understanding Means Peace
20 November 1943		Open Discussion: Toyohiko Kagawa — Key Saying: "Religion is the Whole Life in Action" (Kagawa)
27 November 1943	Mr N. M. Bell	The Miraculous in Religion
11 December 1943	Mr S. Schofield	Christian Order: To Be or Not to Be
20 December 1943		Social Event
5 February 1944	Mr N. M. Bell	Is a Free Religious Movement Needed?
12 February 1944	Mr N. M. Bell	From Instinctive to Cosmic Living
19 February 1944	Mr N. M. Bell	God and the Soul Today

Appendix 4

Date	Speaker	Topic
26 February 1944		Open Discussion: Man and Woman Today
4 March 1944	Mr N. M. Bell	Glands Regulating Personality, or How to Change Human Nature
11 March 1944	Mr N. M. Bell	From Eros to Agape, or from Love to Love
18 March 1944	Mr N. M. Bell	Can Man Forgive God?
25 March 1944	Mr N. M. Bell	The Dead as Unifiers of the Living
8 April 1944	Mr N. M. Bell	The Symbolism of the Dying God
29 April 1944	Mr N. M. Bell	From Cannibalism through Exploitation to Brotherhood
6 May 1944	Mr N. M. Bell	The Atlantic Charter in the Light of World Brotherhood
20 May 1944	Mr N. M. Bell	What is the Meaning of My Life? Tolstoy's Answer
27 May 1944	Mr N. M. Bell	Significant Events in USA History
10 June 1944	Mr N. M. Bell	Freedom Through Fraternity
24 June 1944	Mr N. M. Bell	The Life and Work of Abraham Lincoln
22 July 1944	Mr N. M. Bell	Armageddon: its Original Meaning and Present-day Significance
29 July 1944	Mr N. M. Bell	To Travel Hopefully is Better than to Arrive
5 August 1944	Mr B. R. McLaren	Liberalism

Free Religious Movement Lectures

Date	Speaker	Topic
19 August 1944	Mr N. M. Bell	Can Faith Heal?
26 August 1944	Mr N. M. Bell	"I Teach You the Superman" (Nietzsche)
2 September 1944	Mr N. M. Bell	Seeing Life Whole
9 September 1944	Mr N. M. Bell	How Should We Regard the State?
16 September 1944	Mr N. M. Bell	Africa's World Problem
23 September 1944	Mr N. M. Bell	Lin Yutang Looks at Life
14 October 1944	Mr N. M. Bell	The World of the Unborn
18 November 1944	Mr N. M. Bell	East and West
25 November 1944	Mr N. M. Bell	Basic Christianity as a World Religion
2 December 1944	Mr N. M. Bell	Is the Family our Only Religious Institution?
9 December 1944	Mr N. M. Bell	Basic Buddhism and Basic Christianity Compared

Notes and Bibliography

Notes

Introduction

1 See Matthew 13:57, Mark 6:4, Luke 4:24, John 4:44.

2 *New York Times,* 1 December 1881, p. 4.

3 Rachel Buchanan, "Why Gandhi Doesn't Belong at Wellington Railway Station", *Journal of Social History* (Summer 2011), pp. 1077-1093.

4 Archibald Baxter (1881-1970) wrote an essay on his wartime experiences as a pacifist conscript who suffered field punishment, which was published in Harry E. Holland, *Armageddon or Calvary: The Conscientious Objectors of New Zealand and "The Process of Their Conversion"* (Wellington: Maoriland Workers Printing and Publishing Company, 1919), pp. 75-87. Later he wrote his autobiography, *We Will Not Cease* (London: Victor Gollancz, 1939), although most of the copies of the book were destroyed in the London Blitz in 1941. The book went on to become a New Zealand classic, reprinted by Penguin Books and rarely out of print. The most recent edition, with a foreword by Michael King, was published by Eddie Tern Press in the United States in 2000.

5 Mark Bostridge, *Vera Brittain and the First World War: The Story of* Testament of Youth (London: Bloomsbury, 2014) tells how *Testament of Youth* was written and published in 1933, the development of Vera Brittain's pacifist ideas and her decision to become a sponsor of the Peace Pledge Union in 1937. Finally it describes the production of a major film based on the book.

6 Robin Hyde, *Passport to Hell* (Auckland: Auckland University Press, 2015). Many of Robin Hyde's other works are online in electronic format.

7 Ralph Waldo Emerson, *Journal,* May 28, 1839.

8 Thirty-third Annual Report of the Minister of Education, *Higher Education,* presented to both Houses of the General Assembly of the New Zealand Parliament, 1910.

Notes

⁹ James Hight and Alice M. F. Candy, *A Short History of the Canterbury College (University of New Zealand) With a Register of Graduates and Associates of the College* (Christchurch: Whitcombe and Tombs Limited, 1927), p. 246.

¹⁰ W. J. Gardner, E. T. Beardsley, and T. E. Carter, *A History of the University of Canterbury 1873-1973* (Christchurch: University of Canterbury, 1973).

¹¹ Gardner, et al., *A History of the University of Canterbury 1873-1973*, p. 91.

¹² It appears to be the same oversight that has left Norman Murray Bell from being listed amongst the Christ's College alumni. The old boys' magazine *Quadrangle*, May 2003, no. 28 has a brief article on N. M. Bell, entitled "A Forgotten Scholar": "[O]ne whose name is virtually forgotten, although his record stretches the limits of credulity..." After recounting his academic achievements the author expected that he would have had "a glittering career" in academia and is surprised that Bell became a self-employed examination tutor. What is equally surprising is the author's failure to discover that the reason for this was Bell's pacifism and imprisonment during the war, which led to the deprivation of his civil rights for a further ten years and disqualification from holding any government-related employment.

¹³ Catherine Amey, *The Compassionate Contrarians: A History of Vegetarians in Aotearoa New Zealand* (Wellington: Rebel Press, 2014), pp. 84-98.

¹⁴ Both quotations are in Charles R. Joy (ed.), *Albert Schweitzer: An Anthology* (London: Adam and Charles Black, 1952), pp. 262, 265.

¹⁵ Bell provided an account of this experience in "Hallucination or Illumination: Psychology of Ecstatic Vision", notes for a talk to the Practical Psychology Club, October 1931. Christchurch City Libraries Archive 280, Ms 86.

¹⁶ *The Dominion*, 28 March 1911, p. 4. Social Darwinism swept the western world in the early twentieth century and New Zealand was no exception. Eugenics societies advocated encouraging the birth rate of those considered healthy and fit while discouraging reproduction amongst the "feeble-minded".

¹⁷ *Cambridge University Calendar for the year 1910-1911* (Cambridge: Deighton Bell & Co., 1910), pp. 1080-1083.

¹⁸ *The University of Liverpool Calendar, 1914*, p. 532, records that Norman Murray Bell was a research student in residence in the Faculty of Science.

¹⁹ Meeting of the Board of Governors of Canterbury College reported in *The Press*, 27 February 1917, p. 2.

²⁰ New Zealand Defence Force Personnel Records, Norman Murray Bell, Archives New Zealand Reference WW1 64795-Army.

Notes

Chapter 1: A Dissenting Heritage and the Challenge of Orthodoxy

1   Most of the Albertland settlers (over 1500) arrived in 1862 and 1863, with a further 400 in 1864 and 500 in 1865. Not all of the passengers in the later years were destined for Albertland; for example the *Victory* arrived on 4 January 1865 carrying 247 passengers, of which about a third (80) intended settling at Albertland. See Appendix 1 for details.

2   *The Illustrated London News*, 7 June 1862.

3   "The Albertlanders", *Auckland Star*, 13 June 1925, p. 27.

4   *New Zealand Gazette and Wellington Spectator*, 4 September 1844, p. 3.

5   See Appendix 2 for the location of the Albertland Settlement on the Kaipara Harbour.

6   *Albertland Gazette*, 1 October 1863, p. 4.

7   Dick Scott, *Seven Lives on Salt River* (Auckland: Reed Books, 1999), p. 16.

8   Samuel Edger, *Sermons Preached at Auckland, New Zealand* (London: Yates & Alexander, 1869), p. vii.

9   H. Mabbett, *Wellsford — Tidal Creek to Gum Ridge* (Wellsford: Lower North Weekly News, 1968), p. 273.

10   Lee Sands, Records and Archives Department, British Medical Association, personal communication, 30 January 2018.

11   Information contained in the Death Printout from the Department of Births, Deaths and Marriages for Henrietta Bell, died 15 April 1913 at Port Albert. A handwritten note from Dr Bell's grandson found in the Albertland Settlers Museum archives says Henrietta and James married at an unnamed Cathedral in Hong Kong. This later, orally transmitted story is less likely to be accurate than the death record in 1913.

12   Rex Earl Wright-St Clair, *Historia Nunc Vivat: Medical Practitioners in New Zealand 1840-1930* (Christchurch: Cotter Medical History Trust, 2013).

13   Jane Wordsworth, *Women of the North* (Auckland: Collins, 1981), p. 26.

14   J. L. Borrows, *Albertland* (Wellington: A.H. & A.W. Reed, 1969), pp. 133-134.

15   Mabbett, *Wellsford — Tidal Creek to Gum Ridge*, p. 273.

16   Death Printout from the Department of Births, Deaths and Marriages for James Bell, died 9 August 1870.

17   *Daily Southern Cross*, 5 September 1870, p. 2.

18   *New Zealand Herald*, 26 January 1891, p. 10; and 11 May 1896, p. 5. The Suffrage Petition Roll-Sheet 383, Region: Te Aroha.

19   *The Press*, 20 July 1898, p. 4.

20   David Hackett Fischer, *Fairness and Freedom: A History of Two Open Societies: New Zealand and the United States* (New York: Oxford University Press, 2012), p. 56. Hackett records that Edward Gibbon Wakefield did not approve of the Oxford Movement "and thought it was moving in the wrong direction," p. 59.

21   *The Christ's College Ordinance* passed by the Canterbury Provincial Council on 27 June 1855.

22   "Introduction to the School", *Christ's College Grammar School*, Christmas 1900.

23   *The Press*, 18 December 1901, p. 8.

24   Jane Teal, personal communication.

25   James Hight and Alice M.F. Candy, *A Short History of Canterbury College*, (Auckland: Whitcombe and Tombs, 1927), p. 246.

26   *The Press*, 3 April 1909, p. 9.

27   *New Zealand Herald*, 4 September 1909, p. 6.

28   Thirty-third Annual Report of the Minister of Education, *Higher Education*, presented to both Houses of the General Assembly of the New Zealand Parliament, 1910, p. 19.

Chapter 2: Intellectual Development

1   *The Cambridge University Calendar for the year 1910-1911* (Cambridge: Deighton Bell and Co., 1910); and *The Cambridge University Calendar for the year 1912-1913* (Cambridge: Deighton Bell and Co., 1912).

2   Norman Murray Bell, "On the Velocity of Evolution of Oxygen from Bleaching-Powder Solutions in the Presence of Cobalt-Nitrate and the Modifications produced by the Additions of Various Compounds", *Transactions and Proceedings of the Royal Society of New Zealand* 43 (1910), pp. 26-28.

3   In 1898 Ernest Rutherford returned to New Zealand to marry his fiancée Mary Newton, at the Anglican Church at Papanui, Christchurch. The couple then travelled to Montreal, Canada where Rutherford took up a professorship. In 1907 Rutherford became professor of physics at Manchester University where by 1917 his research led to the splitting of the atom. In 1919 he became Director of the Cavendish Laboratory, Professor of Experimental Physics and was elected a

Notes

Fellow of Trinity College. During the war, foreseeing the promise and the peril in atomic power, he expressed the hope that the energy from the atom would not be extracted until humankind lived in peace. He visited his homeland on four occasions, the last in 1925 where he gave public talks in the main cities of New Zealand. In 1931 he was given a peerage, becoming Lord Rutherford of Nelson. He died in 1937 from complications following a hernia operation and his ashes were buried in the nave of Westminster Abbey. Nuclear fission, which led to nuclear power, was discovered two years after his death. Emma Brewerton, "Ernest Rutherford Biography", New Zealand History Online, https://nzhistory.govt.nz/people/ernest-rutherford; and "Ernest Rutherford-Facts", NobelPrize.org, https://www.nobelprize.org/prizes/chemistry/1908/rutherford/facts

4   W. C. Lubenow, *The Cambridge Apostles 1820-1914: Liberalism, Imagination, and Friendship in British Intellectual and Professional Life* (Cambridge: Cambridge University Press, 1998), p. 240.

5   Daniela Donnini Maccio, "Ethics, economics and power in the Cambridge Apostles' internationalism between the two world wars", *European Journal of International Relations*, 22:3 (2015), pp. 696-721.

6   Bertrand Russell was convicted of writing a pamphlet supporting conscientious objection for the No Conscription Fellowship. He was fined £100, which he did not pay, so his goods at Cambridge were seized and sold to pay the fine. (Most of them were bought by his friends and later returned to him.) The Trinity College Council agreed unanimously on 11 July 1916 to remove him from his College lectureship. In 1918 he published an article criticising the involvement of American troops in the war and was sentenced to six months imprisonment. He was appointed to a College lectureship in 1930, but it was not until 1944, when Trinity College elected Russell to an honorary fellowship, that amends were made.

7   Geoffrey F. Nutall, *New College London and its Library* (London: Dr Williams Trust, 1977), p. 8 n.7.

8   Roger Tomes, "'Learning a New Technique': The Reception of Biblical Criticism in the Nonconformist Colleges," *The Journal of the United Reformed Church Historical Society* 7:5 (2004), pp. 288-314.

9   University of London, Register of Boards of Studies (Theology), September 1912.

10   University of London, Regulations Relating to the Degrees in Theology For External Students, 1912, pp. 2-8.

11   University of London Enrolment Card 26577 Bell, Norman Murray. B.D. 1st. cl. Hons. Study of Religion 1915.

Notes

12   Dr Walter Walsh, "From Presbyterian Dogma to Universal Religion", address in the Kinnaird Hall, Dundee, 10 November 1912.

13   Sometimes the heresy of today becomes the orthodoxy of tomorrow when tomorrow is a century later. For example, in 1963 the Anglican Bishop of Woolwich, John A.T. Robinson (1919-1983), wrote *Honest to God,* which sought to restate traditional orthodoxy in modern terms, based upon the works of European theologians Paul Tillich, Dietrich Bonhoeffer, and Rudolf Bultmann. The book became hugely popular, selling over a million copies. It was radical, appeared to contradict many basic Anglican tenets, to some was heretical, and was criticised by orthodox theologians; yet Bishop Robinson faced no heresy charge. N. T. Wright, "Doubts about Doubt: *Honest to God* Forty Years On", *Journal of Anglican Studies* 3:2 (2005), pp. 181-195.

In 1967 the General Assembly of the Presbyterian Church of New Zealand charged Lloyd Geering, Principal of Knox Theological Hall and Professor of Old Testament studies, with doctrinal error and disturbing the peace and unity of the church. Like the charges against Voysey, these charges were whipped up by the actions of the Layman's Association. Geering was acquitted in what was popularly known as the "heresy trial", and Sir Lloyd Geering has now become in the public mind New Zealand's prophet of modernity and a public intellectual of great esteem. He is also a life-long pacifist. Paul Morris and Mike Grimshaw (eds.), *The Lloyd Geering Reader* (Wellington: Victoria University Press, 2007), pp. 8-22.

14   Warren Sylvester Smith, *The London Heretics 1870-1914* (London: Constable, 1967), pp. 127-130.

15   Lionel Carey, *Edvard Grieg in England* (Woodbridge: Boydell Press, 2006), pp. 126-127.

16   Walter Walsh, *The Moral Damage of War* (London: R. Brimley Johnson, 1902).

17   Stow Persons, *Free Religion: An American Faith* (New Haven: Yale University Press, 1947), pp. 42-43.

18   Adin Ballou was the leader of the Hopedale community in Massachusetts (1841-1856). During the Civil War he was nearly alone amongst the abolitionists in maintaining his pacifist principles. He left a remarkable moral legacy, late in his life corresponding with the Russian pacifist Leo Tolstoy who in turn was an influential thinker for Gandhi, whose fountain of ideas about peace and non-violent resistance would be seminal for Martin Luther King Jr. Lynn Gordon Hughes, introduction to Adin Ballou, *Christian Non-Resistance* (Providence, RI: Blackstone Editions, 2006), pp. xxiii-xxiv. On Ballou's relationship with the Universal Peace Union see Lynn Gordon Hughes (ed.), *Autobiography of Adin Ballou: Annotated Edition* (Toronto: Blackstone Editions, 2016), pp. 321, 534 n. 25.

Notes

[19] N. M. Bell, *A Gospel of Universal Compassion Being Another Side of Christianity* (Christchurch: printed by I.M. Isitt, n.d. [c.1916]). Norman Murray Bell said he completed the work about the middle of the year.

[20] See *Otago Daily Times*, 30 March 1918, p. 2; and *Otahuhu Standard*, 30 January 1923, p. 3.

[21] G. W. Roderick and M. D. Stephens, "The Development of Science and Technology in a Civic University: Liverpool 1881-1914", *The Irish Journal of Education* ix:2 (1975), pp. 77-96.

[22] The University of Liverpool Calendar, 1914, p. 532.

[23] N. M. Bell, "Uber die Geschwindigkeit der Sauerstoffentwickelung aus Chlorkalkosungen bei Gegenwart kleiner Nengen von Kolbalt-nitrat, und uber den Einfluß verschiedener Verbindungen auf diese", *Zeitschrift Anorganische Chemie* 82 (1913), pp. 145-163. The paper gave Bell's institution as Muspratt Laboratory, University of Liverpool. I am grateful to David Ross for drawing my attention to this paper.

[24] Alfred Holt and Norman Murray Bell, "The System m-Xylene-Ethyl Alcohol-Water", *Journal of the Chemical Society Transactions* 105 (1914), pp. 633-639.

[25] Andrew Carnegie, *A League of Peace* (Boston: The International Union, 1906).

[26] University of St Andrews, Minutes of the meeting of Academic Senate, 7 November 1914.

[27] N. M. Bell, *Education For Freedom* (Greymouth: Grey River Argus Co., 1921).

[28] *The Press*, 8 September 1915, p. 8.

[29] The Faraday Society merged in 1980 with several similar institutions, including the Chemical Society and the Society for Analytical Chemistry, to form the Royal Society of Chemistry.

[30] Norman Murray Bell, "On the Anodic Solution of Lead", *Transactions of the Faraday Society* 11 (1915), pp. 79-90.

[31] *The Sun*, 8 September 1915, p. 4.

[32] *The Press*, 31 May 1915, p. 7.

[33] The University of Heidelberg searched their archives and could not find a student file for Norman Murray Bell, which meant he did not matriculate at that university. If he informally audited a course there would be no record. Sabrina Zinke, personal communication 16 September 2014.

[34] University of Bern archives, personal communication 4 September 2013 and 13 February 2019, confirming that Norman Murray Bell did not sit any examinations.

Chapter 3: War and Resistance

1   Frank Sargeson, *Frank Sargeson's Stories* (Auckland: Cape Catley, 2010), p. 29.

2   Norman Murray Bell, letter to Innes MacGregor, 11 January 1928. Alexander Turnbull Library, PAM 1916 BEL 3584.

3   Charles R. Joy (ed.), *Albert Schweitzer: An Anthology* (London: Adam and Charles Black, 1952), pp. 189, 252.

4   *Albert Schweitzer: An Anthology*, pp. 290-291.

5   Martin Brecht, *Martin Luther: His Road to Reformation, 1483-1521* (Minneapolis: Fortress Press, 1985), vol. 1, p. 460.

6   It has been argued that the Reformation made a significant contribution to the modern development of personal liberty. A.C. Grayling comments in *Towards the Light: The Story of the Struggles for Liberty & Rights in the Modern West* (London: Bloomsbury, 2007), p. 18, that a "more accurate way of looking at it is to see the effort made by a diversity of people to escape the hegemony of the Church as being in truth, about many kinds of liberty, not just liberty of conscience and worship." However, Lynn Hunt, in *Inventing Human Rights: A History* (New York: W. W. Norton, 2007), makes the case that the French and Americans revolutions led to the spread of the idea of universal human rights which applied to all people.

7   Aleksandar S. Santrac, "The Legacy of Martin Luther's *Sole Fide*", *In die Skriflig* 51:1 (2017), a2775, https://doi.org/10.4102/ids.v51i1.2275.

8   Brian Bond, "The 'Just War' in Historical Perspective", *History Today* 2 (1966), pp. 111-119.

9   Gregory M. Reichberg, "Thomas Aquinas Between Just War and Pacifism", *Journal of Religious Ethics* 38 (2010), pp. 219-241.

10 "From the beginning they also proclaimed a peace witness as firm as that of the Quakers, though more subdued." Peter Brock, "The Peace Testimony of the Early Plymouth Brethren," *Church History* 53:1 (1984), pp. 30-45.

11 Peter Brock, *Pacifism in Europe to 1914* (Princeton NJ: Princeton University Press, 1972), pp. 378-391.

12 Susan Niditch, *War in the Hebrew Bible A Study in the Ethics of Violence* (New York: Oxford University Press, 1993), pp. 8-9.

13 *Boys' High School Magazine*, No. 55 (April 1917), staff list and p. 2.

14 *The Sun*, 5 July 1917, p. 1; 7 July 1917, p. 15; 14 July 1917, p. 15; 17 July 1917, p. 5.

15 *Maoriland Worker*, 16 April 1917, p.4.

Notes

16 *Maoriland Worker*, 25 July 1917, p.6.

17 Archives New Zealand, New Zealand Defence Force Personnel Records, Norman Murray Bell, WWI 64795-Army.

18 *Evening Post*, 12 September 1927, p. 9.

19 *Evening Post*, 12 September 1927, p. 9.

20 Some writers such as Paul Baker, *King and Country: New Zealanders, Conscription and the Great War*, (Auckland: Auckland University Press, 1988), p. 209, have stated that civil rights were restored a year earlier than originally legislated. This is incorrect. Rights were not restored for ten years; legislative attempts to reduce the period failed.

21 In 1948, Fitzgerald Street was renamed Geraldine Street, but the street numbers remained the same.

22 *The Sun*, 22 April 1919, p. 1.

23 Ian Doughtery, *The People's University: A Centennial History of the Canterbury Workers' Educational Association 1915-2015* (Canterbury University Press, 2015), p. 41.

24 Jim McAloon, "A Political Struggle: Christchurch Labour Politics 1905-1913," *New Zealand Journal of History* 28:1 (1994), pp. 22-40.

25 Mackie Papers, Series 599, Box 17, Folder 63, Canterbury Museum.

Chapter 4: Working for Peace

1 *Maoriland Worker*, 8 August 1923, p. 9.

2 John Fletcher attended a Quaker conference in Wanganui on 11 July 1914, probably in conjunction with his attendance at the Student Christian Movement. He left New Zealand in 1915 and did not return.

3 Lloyd Geering, *Portholes to the Past* (Wellington: Steele Roberts, 2016), pp. 19, 22, 117.

4 Laurie Guy, "Baptist Pacifists in New Zealand", *Baptist Quarterly* 40:8 (2004), pp. 488-499.

5 Laurie Guy, "Early Christian Pacifists in Christchurch: Creating Division in the Fight for Peace", paper presented to Anglican Pacifist Society Meeting in Christchurch, 26 August 2006.

6 Laurie Guy, *Shaping Godzone: Public Issues and Church Voices in New Zealand 1840-2000* (Wellington: Victoria University Press, 2011), p. 262.

7   Charles Henry Cole - WW1 3/1386-Army Reference: AABK 18805 W5530 82/ 0026616.

8   C.H. Cole, "What Will the Baptists Do?", *The New Zealand Baptist*, August 1929, p. 230.

9   Oona Hathaway and Scott J. Shapiro, "Outlawing War? It Actually Worked", *New York Times*, September 2, 2017. Also see the same authors' book *The Internationalists: How a Radical Plan to Outlaw War Remade the World* (New York: Simon & Schuster, 2017).

10 N. M. Bell, "Educative Wireless", *Tomorrow*, 18 March 1936, pp. 27-29.

11 *The Press*, 6 January 1936, p. 4.

12 Originally published in London by Victor Gollancz in 1939, most of this print was destroyed by German bombing. A second edition by The Caxton Press, published in 1968 in Christchurch, finally brought the book to the public.

13 "Fellowship of Pacifist Ministers", *Tomorrow*, 2 October 1935, p. 10.

14 David Grant, *A Question of Faith: A History of the Christian Pacifist Society* (Wellington: Philip Garside Publishing, 2004), p.18.

15 Geoffrey M.R. Haworth, *Marching As To War? The Anglican Church in New Zealand during WW II* (Christchurch: Wily Publications, 2008), p.169.

16 Gerald Chaudron, *New Zealand in the League of Nations: The Beginnings of an Independent Foreign Policy, 1919-1939* (London: McFarland & Co., 2012), pp. 131-139.

17 Peter Simpson, *Bloomsbury South: The Arts in Christchurch 1933-1953* (Auckland: Auckland University Press, 2016), pp. 3-6.

18 Simpson, *Bloomsbury South*, p. 3.

19 Jill Trevelyan, *Rita Angus: An Artist's Life* (Wellington: Te Papa Press, 2008), p. 20.

20 Simpson, *Bloomsbury South*, p. 3.

21 R. S. White, *Pacifism and English Literature: Minstrels of Peace* (Basingstoke: Palgrave MacMillan, 2008). The Bertrand Russell quote is at p. 53 in this book and is taken from Russell's article "War and Non-Resistance," *Atlantic Monthly* 116 (1915), pp. 266-274.

22 Alice Slaverley, "Marketing Virginia Woolf: Women, War, and Public Relations in *Three Guineas*", *Book History* 12 (2009), pp. 295-339.

23 Allen Curnow, "Prophets of Their Time: Some Modern Poets", *The Press*, 20 January 1940, p.14.

Notes

24 Leonard Bell, *Strangers Arrive: Émigrés and the Arts in New Zealand, 1930-1980* (Auckland: Auckland University Press, 2017).

25 M. Hasselmann, "The Unitarian Universalist Church of Berkeley: A History", 1981, https://uucb.org/category/uucb-a-history/. There is no mention of James Chapple in this history.

26 *The Ashburton Guardian*, 18 May 1918, p. 5.

27 *New Zealand Herald*, 23 June 1926, p. 12.

28 Jessica Gerrard, "'Little Soldiers' for Socialism: Childhood and Socialist Politics in the British Socialist Sunday School Movement," *International Review of Social History* 58 (2013), pp. 71-90.

29 *The Star* [Hawera & Normanby Star], 3 August 1922, p. 4.

30 *Auckland Star*, 22 September 1923, p. 6.

31 James H. G. Chapple, *A Rebel's Vision Splendid* (London: C. W. Daniel Company), p. 5

32 Chapple, *A Rebel's Vision Splendid*, p. 5.

33 After the split in the Gilfillan Memorial Church Dr Walsh formed the Church of Today, meeting at the Kinnaird Hall. This is the church Chapple was offered charge of. W. H. Marwick, "Scottish Heretics in the Scottish Churches," *Scottish Church History Society* (1955), pp. 227-239.

34 Letter, 9 December 1927, Rev. Clyde Carr to Rev. William Jellie, saying Norman Murray Bell was in charge of the Christchurch church and had "changed the name to Free Religious Movement". Auckland War Memorial Museum Library, MS 91/72 Series C Folder 6.

35 Letters, 13 December 1928 and 16 April 1929, Rev. Clyde Carr to Rev. William Jellie. Auckland War Memorial Museum Library, MS 91/72 Series C Folder 6.

36 N. M. Bell, "Wanted: A New Religion," *Tomorrow*, 18 December 1935, pp. 7-9.

37 Free Religious Movement Lectures 1934-1944, Appendix 4.

38 *The Press*, 20 December 1941.

39 Vernon Marshall, "Will Hayes: Neglected Champion of Comparative Religion", *Faith and Freedom* 57:158 (2004), pp. 27-32.

40 Norman Murray Bell, *Maori Myths and Rites in the Light of Human Ontogeny: A Physiologico-psychical Contribution to the Study of Religion*. Thesis (D.Litt.),

Canterbury University College, 1928. University of Canterbury Library Catalogue. The copy deposited in the Christchurch City Libraries, Archive 280, has 256 pages compared to the 274 page copy in the University of Canterbury Library. This may explain the absence of a conclusion in the former.

41   The Will of Norman Murray Bell, dated 24 March 1961 with Codicil of the same date, provided for the distribution of his books amongst the University of Canterbury Library, Christchurch Public Library, Post-Primary schools libraries and the Workers' Educational Association. The Codicil removed the obligation of his Trustees to distribute the dissertation widely to named libraries. The dissertation and related material went into the Christchurch Public Library. Donations were made to the Esperanto Association, Christian Pacifist Society and Australian Pacifist Council. His half share of the family home was, upon his sister's death, to be spent on monthly advertisements for the next 30 years in the Christchurch *Press* and Christchurch *Star* aimed at securing peace between humans and domesticated animals.

42   Norman Murray Bell, "Hallucinations & Illumination: Psychology of Ecstatic Vision", notes for a talk to the Psychological Society, October 1931. (The notes were written on 9 February 1931, two months after the experience occurred.) Christchurch City Libraries Archive 280, Ms 86.

43   *The Compact Edition of the Oxford English Dictionary* (Oxford: Oxford University Press, 1971), vol. A-O, p. 832.

44   William James, *The Varieties of Religious Experience,* first delivered as the Gifford Lectures on Natural Religion at the University of Edinburgh, 1901-1902.

45   John Trevor, *My Quest for God* (London: Labour Prophet, 1897), pp. 256-257.

46   Bertrand Russell, *The Autobiography of Bertrand Russell* (London: Routledge Classics, 2009), pp. 136-137.

47   D. B. Yaden, J. Haidt, R. W. Hood, D.R. Vago & A. B. Newberg, "The Varieties of Self-Transcendent Experience", *Review of General Psychology*, Advanced online publication. http://dx.doi.org/10.1037/gpr000102

48   Catherine Amey, *The Compassionate Contrarians: A History of Vegetarians in Aotearoa New Zealand* (Wellington: Rebel Press, 2014), pp. 84-90.

Chapter 5: The Second World War and Its Aftermath

1   Allan Thomas, "Centennial Music" in William Renwick (ed.), *Creating A National Spirit: Celebrating New Zealand's Centennial* (Wellington: Victoria University Press, 2004), pp. 232-245.

Notes

2   Doug Munro, "J.W. Davidson on the Home Front" in Geoffrey Gray, Doug Munro and Christine Winter (eds.), *Scholars at War: Australasian Social Scientists, 1939-1945* (Canberra: ANU Press, 2012), p. 192.

3   According to her biographer, "Rita's decision to feature a portrait of the English composer in her new painting may have been a not-so-subtle piece of propaganda in her campaign to win Lilburn over to the pacifist cause... Her inclusion of Vaughan Williams in one of her largest works to date was a powerful reminder that some of the most highly respected figures in contemporary music shared her convictions." Jill Trevelyan, *Rita Angus: An Artist's Life* (Wellington: Te Papa Press, 2008), p. 178.

4   *Auckland Star*, 20 January 1940, p. 8.

5   Srinjoy Bose, "Students or Soldiers? Conscientious Objection during World War II" in *Tower Turmoil: Character & Controversies at the University of Otago* (Department of History, University of Otago, 2005), pp. 81-94. The University Senate decided not to provide examination centres in defaulters' camps and the Medical Faculty said conscientious objectors who refused to serve in the Medical Corps should not be enrolled in a later year.

6   David Grant, *Out in the Cold: Pacifists and Conscientious Objectors in New Zealand during World War II* (Auckland: Reed Methuen, 1986), p. 76.

7   David Grant, *Out in the Cold*, p. 76 says that pacifists were able to hold public meetings in Christchurch until late in January 1940. J.E. Cookson, "Pacifism and Conscientious Objection in New Zealand" in Peter Brock and Thomas P. Socknat (eds.), *Challenge to Mars: Essays on Pacifism from 1918 to 1945* (Toronto: University of Toronto Press, 1999), pp. 292-311, says meetings seem "to be have lasted to the war's end" but only cites sources till 1943; see footnote 24, p. 308. This claim is mistaken. See note 8 below.

8   *The Press*, 27 January 1940, p. 10, reports a public meeting in Victoria Square, from which the police rescued the speakers. *The Press*, 30 January 1940, p. 6, has an account of the Christchurch City Council meeting which heard submissions about the disruptive meeting and then revoked the pacifists' meeting permit.

9   Nan Taylor, "Human Rights in World War II in New Zealand", *New Zealand Journal of History* 23:2 (1989), pp. 109-123.

10 David Grant, "The Reverend Ormond Burton and his Antagonists during the Second World War" in Geoffrey Troughton (ed.), *Saints and Stirrers: Christianity, Conflict and Peacemaking in New Zealand 1814-1945* (Wellington: Victoria University Press, 2017), p. 213.

Notes

11   H. Winston Rhodes, *A Memoir: Frederick Sinclaire* (Christchurch: University of Canterbury, 1984), p. 122.

12   Catherine Amey, *The Compassionate Contrarians: A History of Vegetarians in Aotearoa New Zealand* (Wellington: Rebel Press, 2014), pp. 91-92.

13   Walter Walsh, *The World Rebuilt* (London: George Allen & Unwin, 1917), Preface.

14   N. M. Bell, *The Press*, 21 December 1944, p. 6.

15   Paul Tillich, *Systematic Theology* (Chicago: University of Chicago Press, 1981), vol.1, p. 237.

16   N. M. Bell, *The Press*, 7 December 1943, p. 6.

17   N. M. Bell, *The Press*, 21 September 1942, p. 6.

18   N. M. Bell, *The Press*, 11 March 1942, p. 3.

19   N. M. Bell, *The Press*, 26 April 1944, p. 6.

20   N. M. Bell, *The Press*, 8 May 1940, p. 12.

21   N. M. Bell, *The Press*, 4 October 1945, p. 6.

22   Colin Spencer, *The Heretic's Feast: A History of Vegetarianism* (London: Fourth Estate, 1993), p. 296.

23   "Abolition of Death Penalty Request made to Prime Minister," *The Press*, 17 February 1938, p. 9.

24   "Mental Hospitals Board of Inquiry Urged," *The Press*, 17 November 1937, p. 5.

25   Jenny Robin Jones, *Writers in Residence: A Journey with Pioneer New Zealand Writers* (Auckland: Auckland University Press, 2004), p. 281.

26   *The Press*, 29 November 1941, p. 12.

27   Elsie Locke, *Peace People: A History of Peace Activities in New Zealand* (Christchurch: Hazard Press, 1992), p. 162.

28   See the biography by Maureen Birchfield, *Looking for Answers: A Life of Elsie Locke* (Christchurch: Canterbury University Press, 2009).

29   Locke, *Peace People*, p. 161.

30   Locke, *Peace People*, p. 161.

31   Maureen Birchfield, *Looking for Answers*, p. 308.

Notes

32 "Sound: Oxford Union debate on nuclear weapons", https://nzhistory.govt.nz/media/sound/oxford-union-debate, (Ministry for Culture and Heritage), updated 27 July 2017.

33 Paul Morris, Mike Grimshaw (eds)., *The Lloyd Geering Reader* (Wellington: Victoria University Press, 2007), p. 11.

34 Morris et al. (eds), *The Lloyd Geering Reader*, pp. 355, 356.

35 This is a paraphrase of a longer passage written by Theodore Parker (1810-1860), a Transcendentalist minister who called for the abolition of slavery. "I do not pretend to understand the moral universe, the arc is a long one, my eye reaches but little ways. I cannot calculate the curve and complete the figure by the experience of sight; I can divine it by conscience. But from what I see I am sure it bends towards justice." Theodore Parker, *Of Justice and the Conscience* (Boston: Crosby, Nichols & Co, 1853), p. 66.

36 Locke, *Peace People,* p. 162.

37 T. S. Eliot, "Burnt Norton," in *Collected Poems 1909-1935* (London: Faber & Faber, 1942).

Afterword

1 Charles Eddis, "William Phillip Jenkins", in the Dictionary of Unitarian and Universalist Biography, an on-line resource of the Unitarian Universalist History and Heritage Society, https://uudb.org/articles/williamphillipjenkins.html. Charles Eddis was a Canadian peace activist known to Ross. See the Larry Ross Papers. University of Canterbury, MB 1417, Box 61 item 13.

2 Larry Ross interviews with Ruth Greenaway, 2 and 9 June 2003. Unpublished transcript.

3 Larry Ross interviews with Ruth Greenaway.

4 Larry Ross interviews with Ruth Greenaway.

5 George N. Marshall, "The Religious Liberalism of Albert Schweitzer", *The Crane Review* 5 (1963), pp. 3-16.

6 Larry Ross interviews with Ruth Greenaway.

7 Administered under the Eastwoodhill Trust Act 1975, the first arboretum plantings were made in 1918. The founder, Douglas Cook, made tremendous efforts after World War II to plant northern hemisphere species because of the threat of nuclear war. By comparison, the Svalbard Global Seed Vault in the Norwegian arctic opened in 2008; it is based on an earlier frozen seed bank begun in 1984. Although a different operation to Eastwoodhill, both are motivated by

concern of a global crisis which could wipe out plant life forms. Svalbard is experiencing problems with water intrusion as global temperatures rise.

8   M. J. Salinger, "Nuclear winter: impacts on the growing season in New Zealand", *Journal of the Royal Society of New Zealand* 16:4 (1986), pp. 319-333.

9   New Zealand Rationalist Association membership records show their date of joining as 8 June 1962, with an address on the North Shore, Auckland. Membership continued until 1969, with a hiatus until Larry became a financial member again in 1984-1985.

10   Larry Ross, "Bertrand Russell — Philosopher, Author and Peace Activist", comment dated May 14, 2007, on web site *Nuclear-Free Peacemaker New Zealand*. A note on the main page of the site states: "This website was discontinued in 2007 when Larry Ross, the founder/secretary of the NZ Nuclear Free Peacemaking Association fell ill and died 18 April 2012. It has been retrieved in 2016 in order to provide vital information on how New Zealand became a Nuclear Free Zone. It is important as a historic site for research articles on war and peace." https://www.nuclearfree.org.nz/archives/49_Peace-Lovers-and-Activists/Peacelovers.htm.

11   Larry Ross, "World War III and New Zealand", *New Zealand Rationalist*, September/October 1962, pp. 7-8. A footnote records that the family is now settled in Christchurch and that Larry is writing on a major work on "The Probability of War and the Possibility of Peace," which became *World War III and the Southern Hemisphere*. This 156 page manuscript accompanied his "Open Letter to World Statesmen" in 1963.

12   Linus Pauling, "There Is No Alternative to Peace", *New Zealand Rationalist*, November/December 1962, pp. 9-10.

13   Ross, "Bertrand Russell — Philosopher, Author and Peace Activist".

14   "The Great Debate on Vietnam: Holyoake and Hanan v. Ross", *New Zealand Monthly Review*, September 1965.

15   *Salient*, 18 July 1965, p. 7. *Salient* is the weekly students' magazine of the Victoria University of Wellington Students' Association.

16   SIS Personal Files of Larry Ross, reported in Murray Horton, "Obituary Larry Ross", *Watchdog* 130 (August 2012), p. 7. http://www.converge.org.nz/watchdog/30/17.html. Becoming the subject of SIS reports was unsurprising as Larry had written to the SIS director informing him at the outset of the political activities he intended to pursue, so that his intentions should not be misunderstood as they were entirely lawful.

Notes

17   Horton, "Obituary Larry Ross", p. 10.

18   Horton, "Obituary Larry Ross", p. 16.

19   I am grateful to Trevor Cobeldick for providing details about the Humanist Peace Fellowship and Larry's Humanist of the Year Award.

20   Horton, "Obituary Larry Ross", p. 26. Larry discusses this point in "Larry Ross The Anti-Nuclear Warrior", chapter in Michael Fitzsimons and Nigel Beckford, *With a Passion: The extraordinary passions of ordinary New Zealanders* (Wellington: Fitzsimons Beckford Communications & Design, 2001), p. 31.

21   David Lange, *Nuclear Free: the New Zealand Way* (Auckland: Penguin Books, 1990), p. 108.

22   In 1973 the third Labour government made a successful application to the International Court of Justice for interim protection against French atmospheric nuclear testing in the Pacific. The legal team was led by the Attorney General, Dr Martyn Finlay. To avoid a final decision going against it, France said it would stop atmospheric testing and only test underground. Labour party anti-nuclear policy is well established, going back to the second Labour government which in 1959 supported a UN resolution condemning nuclear tests. The Values party's manifesto in 1972, the year it was formed, opposed all nuclear tests, especially French Pacific tests. Its 1975 manifesto went further, calling for a nuclear free zone in the Pacific, both nuclear and conventional weapons disarmament and the prohibition of nuclear powered vessels in New Zealand.

23   Lange, *Nuclear Free*, p. 149.

24   Larry Ross, "Brief History of the New Zealand Nuclear Free Zone Campaign". Paper delivered at the Asian Peace Research Association Conference, Christchurch, 31 January-4 February 1992.

25   Larry Ross, "Open Letter to New Zealand Members of Parliament and Citizens", *Motive* 4:18 (1963), pp. 11-12.

26   "Dr. Schweitzer's Hibbert lectures", *The Inquirer*, 17 November 1934, pp. 531-532.

27   "Arthur Woolley Vallance", *The Inquirer*, 17 November 1990, p. 11.

28   Elspeth Vallance, "Liberal Religion for a New Millennium", unpublished sermon, n.d.

[29] Larry Ross, "The Dangers of Fundamentalist Beliefs on George Bush and on US Foreign Policy". Address to the Unitarian Universalist Fellowship of Christchurch, 21 March 2004.

[30] In the Unitarian Universalist tradition, observed on or close to 1 April each year, as a celebration of the lives of people whose heresy has led to increased freedom of choice in expression of beliefs and lifestyle.

[31] *The New Zealand Humanist* 101 (Summer 1988), p. 15. The award is usually referred to as the Humanist of the Year Award.

Acknowledgements

[1] Mackie Papers, Series 599, Box 17, Folder 63, Canterbury Museum, Christchurch.

Bibliography

Primary Sources

Manuscripts, Archives, and Other Unpublished Sources

Archives New Zealand. New Zealand Defence Force Personnel Records, Harold Douglas Bell. Archives Reference WW1 12/700-Army.

———. New Zealand Defence Force Personnel Records, Norman Murray Bell. Archives Reference WW1 64795-Army.

———. New Zealand Defence Force Personnel Records, Wilfred Osmund Bell. Archives Reference WW1 68779-Army.

———. New Zealand Defence Force Personnel Records, Charles Henry Cole. WW1 3/1386-Army. Reference: AABK 18805 W5530 82/0026616.

Archives New Zealand, Christchurch Probates. Probate of Norman Murray Bell. Reference R19671047, Agency CAHX, Series 2989, Accession CH171, Box 609, Record No. CH1135/1962.

Bell, Norman Murray. "Hallucination or Illumination: Psychology of Ecstatic Vision", notes for a talk to the Practical Psychology Club, October 1931. Christchurch City Libraries Archive 280, Ms 86.

Ross, Larry. "Brief History of the New Zealand Nuclear Free Zone Campaign". Paper delivered at the Asian Peace Research Association Conference, Christchurch, 31 January-4 February 1992.

———. "The Dangers of Fundamentalist Beliefs on George Bush and on US Foreign Policy". Address to the Unitarian Universalist Fellowship of Christchurch, 21 March 2004.

———. Interviews with Ruth Greenaway, 2 and 9 June 2003. Unpublished transcript.

Bibliography

University of Bern Archives.
University of Heidelberg Archives.
University of Liverpool Archives.
University of London Archives.
University of London. Enrolment Card 26577. Bell, Norman Murray. B.D. 1st. cl. Hons. Study of Religion 1915.
University of New Zealand Archives.
University of St Andrews Archives.
University of St Andrews. Minutes of the meeting of Academic Senate, 7 November 1914.
Vallance, Elspeth. "Liberal Religion for a New Millennium", unpublished sermon, n.d.

Letters

Bell, Norman Murray. Letter to Innes MacGregor, 11 January 1928. Alexander Turnbull Library, PAM 1916 BEL 3584.

Carr, Clyde. Letters to William Jellie, 9 December 1927, 13 December 1928, and 16 April 1929. Auckland War Memorial Museum Library, MS 91/72 Series C Folder 6.

Mackie, Charles and Norman Murray Bell. Correspondence. Mackie Papers, Series 599, Box 17, Folder 63, Canterbury Museum, Christchurch.

Newspapers and Periodicals

Albertland Gazette
Ashburton Guardian
Auckland Star
Daily Southern Cross
Evening Post
Illustrated London News
Maoriland Worker
New Zealand Gazette and Wellington Spectator
Otago Daily Times

Bibliography

Otahuhu Standard
Penny Illustrated Paper (London)
The Dominion
The Press
Salient (weekly students' magazine of the Victoria University of Wellington Students' Association)
The Sun

Books, Pamphlets and Reports

Ballou, Adin. *Autobiography of Adin Ballou* [1896]. Annotated edition edited by Lynn Gordon Hughes. Toronto: Blackstone Editions, 2016.

———. *Christian Non-Resistance* [1846]. Edited by Lynn Gordon Hughes. Providence, RI: Blackstone Editions, 2006.

Baxter, Archibald. *We Will Not Cease*. London: Victor Gollancz, 1939.

Bell, N. M. *A Gospel of Universal Compassion Being Another Side of Christianity*. Printed by I.M. Isitt, Christchurch, n.d. [c. 1916].

———. *Education For Freedom*. Greymouth: Grey River Argus Co., 1921.

Cambridge University Calendar for the year 1910-1911. Cambridge: Deighton Bell & Co., 1910.

Cambridge University Calendar for the year 1912-1913. Cambridge: Deighton Bell & Co., 1912.

Carnegie, Andrew. *A League of Peace*. Boston: The International Union, 1906.

Chapple, James H. G. *A Rebel's Vision Splendid*. London: C. W. Daniel Company, 1924.

Christ's College Ordinance. Passed by the Canterbury Provincial Council, 27 June 1855.

Edger, Samuel. *Sermons Preached at Auckland, New Zealand*. London: Yates & Alexander, 1869.

Emerson, Ralph Waldo. *Journal*, May 28, 1839. https://archive.org/details/journalsralph05emerrich/page/208/mode/2up

Russell, Bertrand. *The Autobiography of Bertrand Russell* [1951-1969]. London: Routledge Classics, 2009.

Sargeson, Frank. *Frank Sargeson's Stories*. Auckland: Cape Catley, 2010.

Bibliography

Thirty-third Annual Report of the Minister of Education, *Higher Education*. Presented to both Houses of the General Assembly of the New Zealand Parliament, 1910.

Trevor, John. *My Quest for God*. London: Labour Prophet, 1897.

University of Liverpool Calendar. Liverpool University Press, 1914.

University of London. Register of Boards of Studies (Theology). September 1912.

———. Regulations Relating to the Degrees in Theology For External Students. 1912.

Walsh, Walter. *The Moral Damage of War*. London: R. Brimley Johnson, 1902.

———. *The World Rebuilt*. London: George Allen & Unwin, 1917.

Woolf, Virginia. *A Room of One's Own* [1929] and *Three Guineas* [1938]. London: William Collins, 2014.

Articles

Baxter, Archibald. "Chapter XVI: Archibald McC. L. Baxter". In H. E. Holland, *Armageddon or Calvary: The Conscientious Objectors of New Zealand and "The Process of Their Conversion"*. Wellington: Maoriland Workers Printing and Publishing Company, 1919. pp. 75–87.

Bell, N. M. "Educative Wireless". *Tomorrow*, 18 March 1936. pp. 27-29.

———. "On the Anodic Solution of Lead". *Transactions of the Faraday Society* 11 (1915). pp. 79-90.

———. "On the Velocity of Evolution of Oxygen from Bleaching-Powder Solutions in the Presence of Cobalt-Nitrate and the Modifications produced by the Additions of Various Compounds". *Transactions and Proceedings of the Royal Society of New Zealand* 43 (1910). pp. 26-28.

———. "Uber die Geschwindigkeit der Sauerstoffentwickelung aus Chlorkalkosungen bei Gegenwart kleiner Nengen von Kolbalt-nitrat, und uber den Einfluß verschiedener Verbindungen auf diese". *Zeitschrift Anorganische Chemie* 82 (1913). pp. 145-163.

———. "Wanted: A New Religion". *Tomorrow*, 18 December 1935. pp. 7-9.

Cole, C. H. "What Will the Baptists Do?". *The New Zealand Baptist* (August 1929). p. 230.

Curnow, Allen. "Prophets of Their Time: Some Modern Poets". *The Press*, 20 January 1940. p. 14.

Bibliography

"Fellowship of Pacifist Ministers". *Tomorrow*, 2 October 1935, p. 10.

Holt, Alfred and Norman Murray Bell. "The System m-Xylene-Ethyl Alcohol-Water". *Journal of the Chemical Society Transactions* 105 (1914). pp. 633-639.

"Introduction to the School". Christ's College Grammar School, Christmas 1900.

[Ministry for Culture and Heritage]. "Sound: Oxford Union debate on nuclear weapons". https://nzhistory.govt.nz/media/sound/oxford-union-debate, updated July 27, 2017.

Pauling, Linus. "There Is No Alternative to Peace", *New Zealand Rationalist*, November/December 1962, pp. 9-10.

Ross, Larry. "Bertrand Russell — Philosopher, Author and Peace Activist", comment dated May 14, 2007, on web site Nuclear-Free Peacemaker New Zealand. https://www.nuclearfree.org.nz/archives/49_Peace-Lovers-and-Activists/ Peacelovers.htm

———. "Open Letter to New Zealand Members of Parliament and Citizens", *Motive* 4:18 (1963), pp. 11-12.

———. "World War III and New Zealand", *New Zealand Rationalist*, September/October 1962, pp. 7-8.

Russell, Bertrand. "War and Non-Resistance". *Atlantic Monthly* 116 (1915). pp. 266-274.

Secondary Sources

Books and Chapters in Books

Amey, Catherine. *The Compassionate Contrarians: A History of Vegetarians in Aotearoa New Zealand*. Wellington: Rebel Press, 2014.

Armstrong, Karen. *Fields of Blood: Religion and the History of Violence*. London: The Bodley Head, 2014.

Baker, Paul. *King and Country: New Zealanders, Conscription and the Great War*. Auckland: Auckland University Press, 1988.

Ballantyne, Tony. *Orientalism and Race: Aryanism in the British Empire*. London: Palgrave MacMillan, 2012.

Bell, Leonard. *Strangers Arrive: Émigrés and the Arts in New Zealand, 1930-1980*. Auckland: Auckland University Press, 2017.

Bell, Rachael, ed. *New Zealand between the Wars*. Auckland: Massey University Press, 2017.

Bibliography

Bennett, Scott H. *Radical Pacifism: The War Resisters League and Gandhian Nonviolence in America, 1915-1963*. Syracuse, NY: Syracuse University Press, 2003.

Birchfield, Maureen. *Looking for Answers: A Life of Elsie Locke*. Christchurch: Canterbury University Press, 2009.

Borrows, J. L. *Albertland*. Wellington: A. H. & A. W. Reed, 1969.

Bostridge, Mark. *Vera Brittain and the First World War: The Story of* Testament of Youth. London: Bloomsbury, 2014.

Brecht, Martin. *Martin Luther: His Road to Reformation, 1483-1521*, volume 1. Minneapolis: Fortress Press, 1985.

Brock, Peter. *Pacifism in Europe to 1914*. Princeton, NJ: Princeton University Press, 1972.

Carley, Lionel. *Edvard Grieg in England*. Woodbridge, Suffolk: Boydell Press, 2006.

Chaudron, Gerald. *New Zealand in the League of Nations: The Beginnings of an Independent Foreign Policy, 1919-1939*. Jefferson, NC: McFarland & Co, 2012.

Collinge, John. *An Identity for New Zealand?* Auckland: Thesaurus Press, 2010.

Cooke, Bill. *Kernel & Husk: The Waning of Jesus in Godzone*. Wellington: Steele Roberts, 2014.

Cookson, J. E. "Pacifism and Conscientious Objection in New Zealand". In Peter Brock and Thomas P. Socknat (eds.), *Challenge to Mars: Essays on Pacifism from 1918 to 1945*. Toronto: University of Toronto Press, 1999.

Crawford, Robert. *Young Eliot: From St Louis to* The Waste Land. London: Jonathan Cape, 2015.

De Vries, Susanna. *Heroic Australian Women in War*. Sydney: Harper Collins Publishers, 2004.

Deery, Phillip and Julie Kimber. *Fighting Against War: Peace Activism in the Twentieth Century*. Melbourne: Leftbank Press, 2015.

Doughtery, Ian. *The People's University: A Centennial History of the Canterbury Workers' Educational Association ,1915-2015*. Christchurch: Canterbury University Press, 2015.

Elsmore, Bronwyn. *Mana from Heaven: A Century of Maori Prophets in New Zealand*. Tauranga: Moana Press, 1989.

Evans, Richard J. *The Pursuit of Power: Europe 1815-1914*. St Ives: Penguin, 2017.

Bibliography

Fischer, David Hackett. *Fairness and Freedom: A History of Two Open Societies, New Zealand and the United States.* New York: Oxford University Press, 2012.

Gardner, W. J., E. T. Beardsley, and T. E. Carter. *A History of the University of Canterbury, 1873-1973.* Christchurch: University of Canterbury, 1973.

Geering, Lloyd. *Portholes to the Past: Reflections on the Early 20th Century.* Wellington: Steele Roberts, 2016.

Grant, David. *Out in the Cold: Pacifists and Conscientious Objectors in New Zealand during World War II.* Christchurch: Wily Publications, 2008.

———. *A Question of Faith: A History of the Christian Pacifist Society.* Wellington: Philip Garside Publishing, 2004.

———. "The Reverend Ormond Burton and his Antagonists during the Second World War". In Geoffrey Troughton (ed.), *Saints and Stirrers: Christianity, Conflict and Peacemaking in New Zealand 1814-1945.* Wellington: Victoria University Press, 2017.

Grayling, A. C. *Towards the Light: The Story of the Struggles for Liberty & Rights that Made the Modern West.* London: Bloomsbury, 2007.

Griffith, Penny. *Out of the Shadows: The Life of Millicent Baxter.* Wellington: PenPublishing, 2015.

Guy, Laurie. *Shaping Godzone: Public Issues and Church Voices in New Zealand, 1840-2000.* Wellington: Victoria University Press, 2011.

Hathaway, Oona, and Scott J. Shapiro. *The Internationalists: How a Radical Plan to Outlaw War Remade the World.* New York: Simon & Schuster, 2017.

Haworth, Geoffrey M. R. *Marching as to War? The Anglican Church in New Zealand during World War II.* Christchurch: Wily Publications, 2008.

Hight, James and Alice M. F. Candy. *A Short History of the Canterbury College (University of New Zealand) With a Register of Graduates and Associates of the College.* Christchurch: Whitcombe and Tombs Limited, 1927.

Hunt, Lynn. *Inventing Human Rights: A History.* New York: W. W. Norton, 2007.

Hyde, Robin. *Passport to Hell.* Edited by D. I. B. Smith. Auckland: Auckland University Press, 2015.

Jacobs, Alan. *The Year of Our Lord 1943: Christian Humanism in an Age of Crisis.* New York: Oxford University Press, 2018.

James, William. *The Varieties of Religious Experience* [1902]. London: The Fontana Library, 1968.

Jones, Jenny Robin. *Writers in Residence: A Journey with Pioneer New Zealand Writers*. Auckland: Auckland University Press, 2004.

Kershaw, Ian. *To Hell and Back: Europe 1914-1949*. St Ives: Penguin, 2016.

Krogt, Christopher J. van der. "Conscience of the Nation? The Churches as Political Actors". In Rachael Bell (ed.), *New Zealand between the Wars*. Auckland: Massey University Press, 2017.

Lange, David. *Nuclear Free: The New Zealand Way*. Auckland: Penguin Books, 1990.

Leadbeater, Maire. *Peace, Power & Politics: How New Zealand Became Nuclear Free*. Dunedin: Otago University Press, 2013.

Locke, Elsie. *Peace People: A History of Peace Activities in New Zealand*. Christchurch: Hazard Press, 1992.

Lubenow, William C. T*he Cambridge Apostles, 1820-1914: Liberalism, Imagination, and Friendship in British Intellectual and Professional Life*. Cambridge: Cambridge University Press, 1998.

Mabbett, H. *Wellsford — Tidal Creek to Gum Ridge*. Wellsford: Lower North Weekly News, 1968.

McGrath, Alister E. and Darren C. Marks, eds. *The Blackwell Companion to Protestantism*. Oxford: Blackwell Publishing, 2004.

Munro, Doug. "J. W. Davidson on the Home Front". In Geoffrey Gray, Doug Munro and Christine Winter (eds.), *Scholars at War: Australasian Social Scientists, 1939-1945*. Canberra: ANU Press, 2012.

Niditch, Susan. *War in the Hebrew Bible: A Study in the Ethics of Violence*. New York: Oxford University Press, 1993.

Norman, Phillip. *Douglas Lilburn: His Life and Music*. Christchurch: Canterbury University Press, 2006.

Nutall, Geoffrey F. *New College London and its Library*. London: Dr Williams Trust, 1977.

Persons, Stow. *Free Religion: An American Faith*. New Haven: Yale University Press, 1947.

Pinker, Steven. *The Better Angels of Our Nature: The Decline of Violence in History and its Causes*. Victoria: Allen Lane/Penguin Australia, 2011.

Rhodes, Winston. *A Memoir: Frederick Sinclaire*. Christchurch: University of Canterbury, 1984.

Bibliography

Ricketts, Harry. *Strange Meetings: The Lives of the Poets of the Great War*. London: Pimlico, 2012.

Rosner, Victoria, ed. *The Cambridge Companion to The Bloomsbury Group*. New York: Cambridge University Press, 2014.

Roth, H. *Pacifism in New Zealand: A Bibliography*. Auckland: University of Auckland Library Bibliographical Bulletin 3, 1966.

Schweitzer, Albert. *Albert Schweitzer: An Anthology*. Edited by Charles R. Joy. London: Adam and Charles Black, 1952.

Scott, Dick. *Seven Lives on Salt River*. Auckland: Reed Books, 1999.

Sell, Alan P. F. *Nonconformist Theology in the Twentieth Century*. Sparkford: Paternoster Press, 2006.

Simpson, Peter. *Bloomsbury South: The Arts in Christchurch 1933-1953*. Auckland: Auckland University Press, 2016.

Smith, Warren Sylvester. T*he London Heretics, 1870-1914*. London: Constable, 1967.

Spencer, Colin. *The Heretic's Feast: A History of Vegetarianism*. London: Fourth Estate, 1993.

Tillich, Paul. *Systematic Theology*, vol. 1 [1951]. Chicago: University of Chicago Press, 1981.

Thomas, Allan. "Centennial Music". In William Renwick (ed.), *Creating A National Spirit: Celebrating New Zealand's Centennial*. Wellington: Victoria University Press, 2004.

Trevelyan, Jill. *Rita Angus: An Artist's Life*. Wellington: Te Papa Press, 2008.

Troughton, Geoffrey, ed. *Saints and Stirrers: Christianity, Conflict and Peacemaking in New Zealand 1814-1945*. Wellington: Victoria University Press, 2017.

Troughton, Geoffrey and Philip Fountain, eds. *Pursuing Peace in Godzone: Christianity and the Peace Tradition in New Zealand*. Wellington: Victoria University Press, 2018.

Waltz, Kenneth N. *Man, The State, and War: A Theoretical Analysis*. New York: Columbia University Press, 2001.

White, R.S. *Pacifism and English Literature: Minstrels of Peace*. Basingstoke: Palgrave MacMillan, 2008.

Wordsworth, Jane. *Women of the North*. Auckland: Collins, 1981.

Wright, E.H., ed. *Bloomsbury Influences: Papers from the Bloomsbury Adaptions Conference, Bath Spa University*. Newcastle upon Tyne: Cambridge Scholars Publishing, 2014.

Wright-St Clair, Rex Earl. *Historia Nunc Vivat: Medical Practitioners in New Zealand 1840-1930*. Christchurch: Cotter Medical History Trust, 2013.

Articles

Bond, Brian. "The 'Just War' in Historical Perspective". *History Today* 2 (1966). pp. 111-119.

Bose, Srinjoy. "Students or Soldiers? Conscientious Objection during World War II". In *Tower Turmoil: Character & Controversies at the University of Otago*. Department of History, University of Otago, 2005.

Brock, Peter. "The Peace Testimony of the Early Plymouth Brethren". *Church History* 53:1 (1984). pp. 30-45.

"Dr. Schweitzer's Hibbert lectures", *The Inquirer*, 17 November 1934, pp. 531-532.

Gerrard, Jessica. "'Little Soldiers' for Socialism: Childhood and Socialist Politics in the British Socialist Sunday School Movement". *International Review of Social History* 58 (2013). pp. 71-90.

"The Great Debate on Vietnam: Holyoake and Hanan v. Ross", *New Zealand Monthly Review*, September 1965.

Guy, Laurie. "Baptist Pacifists in New Zealand". *Baptist Quarterly* 40:8 (2004). pp. 488-499.

———. "Early Christian Pacifists in Christchurch: Creating Division in the Fight for Peace". Paper presented to Anglican Pacifist Society Meeting, Christchurch, 26 August 2006.

Hasselmann, Merv. "The Unitarian Universalist Church of Berkeley: A History". 1981. https://uucb.org/category/uucb-a-history/

Hathaway, Oona, and Scott J. Shapiro. "Outlawing War? It Actually Worked". *The New York Times*, September 2, 2017.

Horton, Murray. "Obituary: Larry Ross", Watchdog 130 (August 2012). http://www.converge.org.nz/watchdog/30/17.html

"John Harris Memorial Collection: A Forgotten Scholar". *Quadrangle* 28 (May 2003).

Bibliography

Maccio, Daniela Donnini. "Ethics, economics and power in the Cambridge Apostles' internationalism between the two world wars". *European Journal of International Relations* 22:3 (2015). pp. 696-721.

Marshall, George N. "The Religious Liberalism of Albert Schweitzer", *The Crane Review* 5 (1963), pp. 3-16.

Marshall, Vernon. "Will Hayes: Neglected Champion of Comparative Religion". *Faith and Freedom* 57:158 (2004). pp. 27-32.

Marwick, W. H. "Scottish Heretics in the Scottish Churches". *Scottish Church History Society* (1955). pp. 227-239.

McAloon, Jim. "A Political Struggle: Christchurch Labour Politics 1905-1913". *New Zealand Journal of History* 28:1 (1994). pp. 22-40.

McLachlan, John. "Arthur Woolley Valance", *The Inquirer*, 17 November 1990, p. 11.

Reichberg, Gregory M. "Thomas Aquinas Between Just War and Pacifism". *Journal of Religious Ethics* 38:2 (2010). pp. 219-241.

Roderick, G. W. and M. D. Stephens. "The Development of Science and Technology in a Civic University: Liverpool 1881-1914". *The Irish Journal of Education* 9:2 (1975). pp. 77-96.

Salinger, M. J. "Nuclear winter: impacts on the growing season in New Zealand", *Journal of the Royal Society of New Zealand* 16:4 (1986), pp. 319-333.

Santrac, Aleksandar S. "The Legacy of Martin Luther's Sole Fide". *In die Skriflig* 51:1 (2017), a2775. https://doi.org/10.4102/ids.v51i1.2275

Slaverley, Alice. "Marketing Virginia Woolf: Women, War, and Public Relations in *Three Guineas*". *Book History* 12 (2009). pp. 295-339.

Taylor, Nan. "Human Rights in World War II in New Zealand". *New Zealand Journal of History* 23:2 (1989).

Tomes, Roger. "'Learning a New Technique': The Reception of Biblical Criticism in the Nonconformist Colleges". *Journal of the United Reformed Church Historical Society* 7:5 (2004). pp. 288-314.

Vallance, Elspeth. "New Life of Schweitzer", *The Inquirer*, 17 July 1976, p. 3.

Wright, N. T. "Doubts about Doubt: *Honest to God* Forty Years On". *Journal of Anglican Studies* 3:2 (2005). pp. 181-195.

Yaden, D. B., J. Haidt, R. W. Hood, D. R. Vago, and A. B. Newberg. "The Varieties of Self-Transcendent Experience". *Review of General Psychology*, advanced online publication. http://dx.doi.org/10.1037/gpr000102

Bibliography

Theses and Research Dissertations

Bell, N. M. (Norman Murray). *Maori myths and rites in the light of human ontogeny: a physiologic[o]-psychical contribution to the study of religious origins.* D. Litt. Thesis, Canterbury University College, 1928.

Shepherd, Charles Leslie. *The Albertland Christian Colonisation Movement.* MA Thesis, Auckland University College, 1942. (Copy held in Auckland City Library.)

Biographical Dictionaries and Other Reference Works

Brewerton, Emma. "Ernest Rutherford Biography". New Zealand History Online. https://nzhistory.govt.nz/people/ernest-rutherford

Eddis, Charles. "William Phillip Jenkins", in the Dictionary of Unitarian and Universalist Biography, an on-line resource of the Unitarian Universalist History and Heritage Society. https://uudb.org/articles/williamphillipjenkins.html

"Ernest Rutherford-Facts". NobelPrize.org. https://www.nobelprize.org/prizes/chemistry/1908/rutherford/facts

Index

Index

ABBREVIATIONS

The following abbreviations are used throughout the Index.

NMB Norman Murray Bell
LR   Larry Ross
FRM Free Religious Movement

Albertland settlement, 9, 14-23; voyages of the Albertland ships, 148-149, 168n.1; map of the Albertland settlement, 150-151
Anabaptists, 60, 61
Anglicans, 9, 15, 27-28, 53, 61, 79, 171n.13. *See also*: Bethell, Ursula; Christ's College; Linzey, Andrew; Selwyn, George; Sinclaire, Frederick; Taylor, Frederick Norman; Thompson, Thurlow; Voysey, Charles
Angus, Rita, 83, 101-102, 178n.3
animal welfare and vegetarianism, xx, 7, 13, 43, 93, 99, 113-114, 119, 124
Anti-Conscription Council, 104-105
anti-nuclear movement, 118-119, 120-121, 123, 130, 132-133. *See also* New Zealand Nuclear Free Zone
Atkinson, Harry, 12, 74, 78, 133
Auckland Unitarian Church. *See under* Unitarian churches and congregations
Australian Pacifist Council, 177n.41
Ballou, Adin, 43, 171n.18
Baptists, 1, 61, 79. *See also*: Brame, William; Cole, Charles; Mackie, Charles; Spurgeon, Thomas
Barrington, Archibald, 79, 103, 108
Baughan, Blanche, 114-115

Baxter, Archibald, 4, 79, 166n.4
Baxter, Millicent Brown, 79
Becroft, John and Sarah, 21, 22
Bell family tree, 152-153
Bell, Annie (Coffey) (NMB mother), xvi, xx, 9, 23, 53
Bell, Florence (NMB aunt), 22
Bell, Harold (NMB brother), 11, 25, 51, 53
Bell, Harold (NMB uncle), 22-23
Bell, Henrietta Mary (NMB grandmother), xvi, xviii, 9, 16, 20, 22-23
Bell, Henry (NMB uncle), 22
Bell, Horace Roland (NMB father), xvi-xvii, xix, xxi, 9, 22, 23, 25, 53, 118
Bell, James (NMB grandfather), xvi, 9, 16, 19-22
Bell, Lucy (NMB aunt), 22
Bell, May (NMB aunt), 22-23
Bell, Norman Murray
  general: literature about, 6-7; photographs of, 24, 34, 54, 116, 117; as a prophet, 2, 120; summary of his career, 1-2, 8-13; timeline, xvi-xxi
  birth, family and ancestry: 9, 22-25
  childhood and youth: 25-27, 29-31. *See also*: Christ's College; Parnell District School; West Lyttelton School
  education: education, 9-11; studies in chemistry, 6, 10, 31, 46, 49-50; in classics, 6, 9-10, 31, 36; in comparative religion, 40-41, 95-96; in education, 6, 10, 48-49; in philosophy of science, 11; in theology, 6, 10-11, 39-40. *See also*: Canterbury University College; University of Bern; University of Cambridge; University of Liverpool;

Index

University of London; University of St. Andrews

peace and anti-war activities: draft resistance, imprisonment, loss of civil rights, 11-12, 43-44, 64-67, 69, 167n.12; leadership in No More War movement, 12-13, 74-80, 103, 117-118; publication of *Cosmos*, 13, 93, 109, 112; opposition to nuclear weapons, 13, 118-119

political views: Labour Party, 69, 111-112; opposition to censorship, 67, 77, 111-112, 117; anticolonialism, 67, 75, 78, 113, 123-124; prison reform, 114-116

religion and philosophy: ecstatic vision, 97-99; reverence for life; 7, 57, 114; theology, 55-56, 93, 110-111; leadership in Unitarian church, Socialist Sunday School, and Free Religious Movement, 89, 91-94, 110, 112, 114; interest in Māori religion, 95-97, 102

teaching: at Christchurch Boys High School, 11, 63; private tutoring, 63, 67; Workers' Educational Association, 67; Canterbury University College, 97

vegetarianism and animal welfare: xx, 7, 13, 43, 93, 99, 113-114, 119, 124

writings: chemistry papers (1910-1915), xvii-xviii, 33, 46, 50; A *Gospel of Universal Compassion* (c.1916), 43-44, 55, 63, 93; *Education for Freedom* (1921), 49; *Maori Myths and Rites* (1928), xix, 95-96, 143-144

Bell, Wilfred (NMB brother), 25, 53
Bell, Winifred (NMB sister), 25, 67, 118
Bertrand Russell Peace Foundation, 133-134
Bethell, Ursula, 82, 114
Bloomsbury Group, 10, 38-39
Bloomsbury South, 81-86. *See also*: Angus, Rita; Bethell, Ursula; Curnow, Allen; Dowling, Basil Cairns; Glover, Denis; Lilburn, Douglas
Bonhoeffer, Dietrich, 110-111, 171n.13
Brame, William Rawson, 16, 19
Brethren, 61
Broadhead, H. D., 97; FRM lecture, 154
Burton, Ormond, 79, 107, 115
Cambridge University. *See* University of Cambridge

Campbell, Archie, 78
Canterbury University College (University of New Zealand): NMB undergraduate studies, xvii, 1, 6-7, 9, 31; D. Litt. thesis, xix, 95-96, 144, 177n.40; teaching and further study, xx, 97. *See also*: Chilton, Charles; Dowling, Basil; Ensom, Sarah; Page, Fred; Rutherford, Ernest; Sinclaire, Frederick; University of Canterbury
Carman, Arther Herbert, 108
Carnegie, Andrew, 47-48
Carr, Clyde, xix, 74, 92
Carrington, Carey John, 109
Caxton Press, 82-85, 106
Chapple, James, xix, 12, 44, 86-92
Chilton, Charles, 37
Christchurch Boys High School, xviii, 11, 63. *See also* Page, Fred
Christchurch Public Library, 143, 177n.41
Christchurch Unitarian Church. *See under* Unitarian churches and congregations
Christian Pacifist Society, 79, 107-108, 177n.41
Christian teachings on war and peace, 58-62
Christ's College, Christchurch, xvii, 1, 9, 26-31, 167n.12
Church of the Larger Fellowship. *See under* Unitarian churches and congregations
Coates, Gordon, 66
Cole, Charles, xix, 74, 78; FRM lectures, 154, 159
Combined Pacifist Committee, xxi, 72, 103
Congregationalists, 15, 61, 79. *See also* Walsh, Walter
conscientious objection, 4, 12, 63-64, 66, 68, 105-108, 178n.5. *See also*: Baxter, Archibald; Hayes, Will; Henderson, Andrew; military defaulters
Conscientious Objectors Fellowship. *See* Fellowship of Conscientious Objectors
Co-operative Press, xxi, 72, 104, 109
Cosmos: A Quarterly Journal of Pacifist Thought, 13, 93, 109, 112, 144-145
Crocker, Brenda, 136, 139
Curnow, Allen, 82-83, 85-86, 120
Curtis, Colin Marshall, 106
Daniel, C. W., 91
Dowling, Basil Cairns, 106
Eddis, Charles, 131

199

Index

Edger, Lilian, 74
Edger, Samuel, 16, 19, 74
Efford, Lincoln, xix, xxi, 71-72, 92, 103-108, 115, 117, 118, 120
Ensom, Sarah and William; Ensom Prize, 77
environmental crisis, 122-123
Esperanto, xx, 67-68, 72, 90, 177n.41
Fellowship of Conscientious Objectors, xix, 12, 68, 105, 108
Fellowship of Pacifist Ministers, 79
First Unitarian Congregation of Toronto. *See under* Unitarian churches and congregations
Fitzroy, Robert, 17
Fletcher, John, 73
Fraser, Peter, 107
Free Religious Association, 42
Free Religious Movement
 in Britain, 11, 12, 41-44, 91
 in New Zealand, xix, 72, 86, 92-95, 110, 112, 114-115; lectures, 154-163
Friends of the Soviet Union, 76
Gandhi, Mohandas, 4, 171n.18
Geering, Lloyd, 73, 122, 171n.13
Gittos, William, xvi, 23
Glover, Denis, 82, 84
Glover, John, 68-69
Godley, John, 27-28
Gospel of Universal Compassion, 43, 55-57, 63, 93, 110
Griffin, Gerald, 80
Haggitt, Percy Bolton, 89
Hall, Richard, 72
Haslam, Francis, 6-7, 35
Hayes, Will (Brother John), 95
Henderson, Andrew Kennaway, 84
Hoare, James O'Bryan, 12
Holt, Alfred, 44-46, 49
Holyoake, Keith, 133-134
Howell, Ronald Charles, 108
Humanist Peace Fellowship, 135
Humanitarian and Anti-Vivisection Society of New Zealand, xx, 99
Hyde, Robin, 5
Ikeda, Daisaku, 4
International Sunbeam. See *Sunbeam*
Irvine, James, 49-50
Jenkins, Bill, 128
Johnson, John, xxi, 103, 106; FRM lecture, 157
Jones, Connie, 107, 115; FRM lecture, 158

Kellogg-Briand Pact, 75-76
Keynes, John Maynard, 10, 37-38
King, Martin Luther Jr, 4, 124, 171n.18
Knight, Percy, 68
Labour Church, 74, 90. *See also* Trevor, John
Labour government, 66, 80-81, 83-84, 92, 108, 112; and Nuclear Free New Zealand, 136-137, 182n.22
Labour Party: New Zealand Labour Party formed, xviii; relations with peace organizations, 70, 76, 78, 118; NMB involvement, xix, 69, 111. *See also* Carr, Clyde; Efford, Lincoln
Lakeshore Unitarian Universalist Congregation (Montreal). *See under* Unitarian churches and congregations
Lamont, Corliss, 128-129
Lange, David, 136-137
League of Nations, 5, 48, 67, 76, 78-79, 80, 113
League of Nations Union, 76-77, 105
Lee, John, 66
Lilburn, Douglas, 82-83, 101-102, 178n.3
Linzey, Andrew, 124
Locke, Elsie, 118-119
London Peace Society, 61
Lowry, Robert, 84-85
Macaskill, Stuart, 138
Mackay, Jessie, 114
Mackie, Charles, xxi, 68, 69, 74, 103, 106, 108, 115, 133
Māori
 NMB interst in, xix, 95-97, 102
 Parihaka community, 2-4, 102
 relations with settlers, land claims, 2-4, 15-16, 19, 100-101, 109, 123-124
Maoriland Worker, 63, 68, 70, 90
Marlborough Unitarian Fellowship. *See under* Unitarian churches and congregations
Martin, Samuel McDonald, 17-18
Martin, William Lee, 92
McCullough, Derek, 139, 141, 142
McDonnell, Edward, 87
Mennonites. *See* Anabaptists
Methodists, 53, 61, 79, 107. *See also*: Burton, Ormond; Jones, Connie; Knight, Percy; Paris, Percy
military defaulters, loss of civil rights, 64-66
Milligan, Robert Roy Douglas, 105, 106

Index

Movement Against War and Fascism, xx, 13, 80
Murray, William Tullibardine, 23
National Peace and Anti-Militarist League, 4
National Peace Conference (1946), 116-117
National Peace Council, xix, 13, 68, 69, 74, 77, 103, 108; relations with No More War Movement, xxi, 70, 76, 78, 117. *See also* Mackie, Charles
Neilson, Peter, 78
New Zealand Freedom League, 72
New Zealand Nuclear Free Zone, 121, 134-139, 182n.22
New Zealand Rationalist Association, 132-133, 158
No Conscription Fellowship, 170n.6
No More War movement, xix-xx, 70-71, 74-79, 80, 90, 103, 117-118
nuclear weapons. *See* anti-nuclear movement; New Zealand Nuclear Free Zone
Our Father's Church, 12
pacifism. *See* peace and pacifism
Page, Fred, xix, 70-71, 89, 92
Page, Sarah, 76-78
Parihaka community, 2-4, 102
Paris, Percy, 70
Parker, Theodore, 180n.35
Parnell District School, xvi, 9
Pauling, Linus, 133
Peace and Anti-Conscription Federation, 104, 118
peace and pacifism
 anti-war literature, 4-5, 166n.5
 peace candidates in New Zealand elections, 106-107, 108
 peace movements in New Zealand: before NMB, 2-5; after NMB, 120-123
peace and pacifism organizations, 61, 104-105. *See also*: Anti-Conscription Council; Bertrand Russell Peace Foundation; Christian Pacifist Society; Combined Pacifist Committee; Fellowship of Conscientious Objectors; Fellowship of Pacifist Ministers; Humanist Peace Fellowship; London Peace Society; Movement Against War and Fascism; National Peace Council; National Peace and Anti-Militarist League; No Conscription Fellowship; No More War movement; Peace and Anti-Conscription Federation; Peace Pledge Union; Peace Union; Plowshares Movement; Student Christian Movement; Universal Peace Union; Voice of Women; War Resisters International; Women's International League for Peace and Freedom
Peace Council. *See* National Peace Council
Peace Pledge Union, 72, 79-80, 103, 117, 166n.5
Peace Union, 117
Plowshares Movement, 123
Practical Psychology Club, xx, 97
Presbyterians, 15, 61, 79, 107. *See also*: Chapple, James; Geering, Lloyd; Murray, William Tullibardine
prison reform, 114-115
Quakers, 15, 43, 61, 72, 118. *See also*: Fletcher, John; Johnson, John; Summers, John
Rhodes, H. Winston, 78, 84, 109
Richardson, Shirley, 130-132, 136
Robinson, John A. T., 171n.13
Ross, Larry
 early life and education, 127-128
 marriage and family, 130-131, 136, See also: Taylor, Sylvia; Richardson, Shirley; Crocker, Brenda
 move to New Zealand, 131-133
 peace and anti-war activities, anti-war activism, 133-135, 139; leadership of Bertrand Russell Peace Foundation, 133-134; Nuclear Free Zone campaign, 135-139
 religion and philosophy, 128-129; addresses to Christchurch UU Fellowship, 140-142
Rotoaira Prison, 64, 69
Russell, Bertrand, 10, 38, 39, 85, 99, 130, 132-133, 170n.6
Rutherford, Ernest, 35-36, 37, 170n.3
Samoan independence movement, 67, 75, 78, 88, 113
Sassoon, Siegfried, 68-69
Saunders, James, 77-79, 104
Savage, Michael, 80-81, 83-84
Schweitzer, Albert, 7, 57, 78, 130, 140
Selwyn, George, 17
Semple, Bob, 70

Index

Sheppard, Dick, 80
Sinclaire, Frederick, 44, 76-77, 84, 93-94, 103, 108-109; FRM lectures, 154, 159
social gospel, 48, 74, 111, 124
Socialist Guild of Youth. *See* Socialist Sunday School
Socialist (Labour) Church, 12
Socialist Sunday School, 71, 89-91, 93, 107
Society for the Promotion of Permanent and Universal Peace, 61
Spanish Civil War, 5, 80
Spurgeon, Thomas, 23
St Andrews University. *See* University of St Andrews
Stout, Robert, 65-66
Student Christian Movement, 73, 76
Sullivan, Daniel, 75, 76, 78
Summers, Connie. *See* Jones, Connie
Summers, John, 107
Sunbeam, 71, 89-90
Taylor, Frederick Norman, 106
Taylor, Sylvia, 130
Te Whiti-o-Rongomai, 2-4
Theistic Church, 11, 41-43
Thompson, Kathleen and Thurlow, xxi, 79, 103, 106
Tillich, Paul, 111, 171n.13
Timaru Unitarian Church. *See under* Unitarian churches and congregations
Tohu Kākahi, 2-4
Tomorrow, 77, 84, 93, 104, 144
Trades and Labour Council, 76
Trevelyan, George Macaulay, 10
Trevor, John, 98-99
Trinity College. *See* University of Cambridge
Unitarians, 12, 15, 43, 44, 61, 72. See also: Carr, Clyde; Chapple, James; Hall, Richard; McCullough, Derek; McDonnell, Edward; Vallance, Elspeth and Arthur
Unitarian churches and congregations
  Auckland Unitarian Church, 72
  Church of the Larger Fellowship, 130
  First Unitarian Congregation of Toronto, 128
  Lakeshore Unitarian Universalist Congregation (Montreal), 131
  Marlborough Unitarian Fellowship, 139-141
  Timaru Unitarian Church, 87-89

Unitarian Progressive Society (Christchurch Unitarian Church), xix, 12, 87-89, 92
Unitarian Universalist Fellowship of Christchurch, 139-142
  See also Free Religious Movement
Unitarian Universalist Fellowship of Christchurch *See under* Unitarian churches and congregations
United Nations, 4, 113, 121, 131, 135
United Nations Association of New Zealand, 133-134
Universal Peace Union, 43, 171n.18
University of Bern, xviii, 6, 11, 51-52
University of Cambridge, xvii-xviii, xxi, 1, 6, 10, 13, 31-32, 33-38, 118, 170n.6
University of Canterbury, 82, 135, 144, 177n.41. *See also* Canterbury University College
University of Liverpool, xviii, 6, 10, 44-46
University of London, xviii, 6, 10-11, 39-40
University of St Andrews, xviii, 6, 10-11, 46-51
Vallance, Elspeth and Arthur, 139-140, 141
Vaughan Williams, Ralph, 102, 178n.3
vegetarianism. *See* animal welfare and vegetarianism
Voice of Women, 131
Voysey, Charles, 41-42
Walsh, Walter, 11, 41-44, 91, 92, 95, 176n.33
War Resisters International, 71, 76-77
WEA. See Workers' Educational Association
Wesleyans, 15. *See also* Gittos, William
West Christchurch District High School, 75
West Lyttelton School, xvii, 27
Whetham, William, 10, 33, 35, 44
Women's Christian Temperance Union, 76
Women's International League for Peace and Freedom, xviii, xxi, 80
Woolf, Virginia, 38, 85
Workers' Educational Association (WEA), xix-xx, 12, 67, 71, 76, 77, 177n.41
World War I, 8, 38-39, 40, 46, 48-51, 53, 55, 62, 88-89; penalties for defaulters, xix, 11-12, 64-67, 96
World War II, 13, 72, 73, 102-109, 112, 116

About the Author

Wayne Facer completed his economics degree at the University of Auckland. Following a number of years in university administration and teaching a community health course in the School of Optometry, he established a health economics consultancy. Later he completed postgraduate studies in history at Massey University. He has written numerous journal articles about bioethical issues, optometry, healthcare reform and history. He is the author of *A Vision Splendid* (2017) and has contributed to the *New Encyclopedia of Unbelief* (2007) and the *Dictionary of Unitarian and Universalist Biography*. Currently, he researches New Zealand Unitarian and freethought history.

www.ingramcontent.com/pod-product-compliance
Lightning Source LLC
Chambersburg PA
CBHW071815080526
44589CB00012B/802